WHAT OTHERS ARE SAYING...

Lorii Myers has three decades of experience as a manager, controller, and business owner. An accomplished woman by the age of thirty, she asserts that the "right attitude" is essential. Targeting Success is the first in a forthcoming series to be published under the 3 Off the Tee brand. Make It Happen, her second title, promises "a current, timely, and thought-provoking journey of self-discovery" that will help readers "develop the right mind-set" for achieving personal success.

Myers' innovative slant will appeal to business-minded individuals who love golf. Her creative advice may benefit any employer, employee, or entrepreneur seeking motivational assistance. Compact and organized, Targeting Success is for busy people who need that special nudge from a competent coach.

ForeWord Clarion Reviews

Let's face it, the world has gone crazy for golf... everyone you speak to today has taken up the game!

Lorii Myers' new book will take you into the world of business through the kaleidoscope of golf. Often we need to look at a problem from a different perspective to see the solution. Myers' approach does just that. The core principles that make an exceptional golfer are the same core principles that make for an exceptional businessperson.

If your objective is a "hole in one" in the business world, then 3 off the Tee: Targeting Success is a must read.

Chris Leader, President, Leader's Edge Training

Extremely positive!

3 Off the Tee: Targeting Success is a modern-day-sports-oriented-healthy-competition approach to achieving success in business and in life.

Myers' wit, enthusiasm, and business smarts will tweak your motivation into high gear. It's one thing to feel encouraged and challenged, but Myers takes it one step further reinforcing the vision of what success really means to the reader.

An undeniable "Trust Your Swing" morale booster!

Sal Occhipinti, President, Corpcom International: Building Partnerships

3Off theTee:

TARGETING SUCCESS

DEVELOP THE **RIGHT BUSINESS ATTITUDE** TO BE **SUCCESSFUL IN THE WORKPLACE**

Lorii Myers

3 Off the Tee: **Targeting Success**

Develop the Right Business Attitude
to Be Successful in the Workplace
Lorii Myers

ii Leda Publishing Corp.

667 Welham Road, Suite 5
Barrie, ON, Canada L4N-0B7

ISBN: 0-9867-9000-1
ISBN-13: 978-0-9867900-0-3
Library of Congress Control Number: 2010902753

Unattributed quotations by Lorii Myers.

Author photograph by Nat Caron Photography.

This book is dedicated to my parents,
Lorne and Dorie Cox,
who have always encouraged me
to chase my dreams
and push beyond the ordinary.

.

Table of Contents

Preface

I love challenge and I am also absolutely passionate about having the guts to go after whatever I want in life. This has sometimes led me down uncertain paths, but I have always become wiser, stronger, and more resilient with any effort I made.

For this reason, I felt compelled to write about the concept of targeting success.

Today's times of uncertainty breed courage, entrepreneurial spirit, and innovation. There is an urgency to step up and take on whatever life throws our way!

We are faced with a two-fold problem: how to self-improve and succeed, and how to thrive through tough economic times. I believe in order to solve those problems, the workplace requires a new way of thinking, and it's motivated by "change-ready" employers and employees who lead the way. These types of people dig in, rebuild, and feed the recovery process. They accept that they can and will make a difference. There is the challenge – making a difference.

But there are a ton of books out there that address these challenges. Why read mine? Knowing what I was up against, I said to myself, if I wanted to write a book, I needed to find an interesting and refreshing way to present the material.

The answer wasn't hard to find. I also am an avid golfer and as I have played hundreds of rounds of golf, I have long thought that golf isn't just a good metaphor for life. It actually presents a great way to structure a book. Why not have you, my readers, go through a round of golf as you read through the advice I give you? What's better than a business book using golf analogies, formatted around the game of golf? It's the perfect match.

So as you read, you will find that you are either on the front nine, the turn, the back nine, or the 19th hole. But golf just doesn't provide the structure. Once I started using golf analogies and personal stories from my thirty-plus years of business experience, the review and discussion of important business concepts and principles took on a new life—relaxed but professional, sophisticated but realistic, and definitely to the point! In golf you don't have much room for error, and that's the way I look at this book.

But there's one thing in golf that always seemed especially metaphoric. It's the "three off the tee" concept. It means that even if you make a bad play, you learn from it and move forward, better than before. Hence the title.

As you read, I want you to think about ways you can target your own success. Accept whatever comes your way. Recognize that you always have choices and decisions to make and that you have to make them. Analyze your best route to get yourself back in play—your "recovery shot"—and go for it!

In closing, I would like to give special thanks to Dr. Patricia Ross of Roberts Ross Publishing who helped me with the original edit and concept of this book. She is a genuine, brilliant talent with a wonderful, creative mind. "What a coach!"

Enjoy *3 Off the Tee: Targeting Success* and accept this challenge:

"Come out to play, take on the world, and make success yours!"

I look forward to hearing your success stories in the very near future!

Hit 'em straight,

Lorii

Email: Lorii@3-Off-the-Tee.com

Introduction

Tee shot. Slice...yikes

*Do I drop a ball or go
three off the tee?*

I regroup and reload.

I'm going for it.

*Deep breath. Loose grip.
Swing thought.*

I'm in the zone...

When you're in this position, you
always have a choice—

you have decisions to make.

I can't begin to tell you how often this happens in golf—especially when you're first learning how to play the game! If you are a golfer, you know exactly what I mean.

For those non-golfers, let me take a minute to explain. A "tee" shot is simply the first shot on a hole where the ball has been shot off a tee. You're at the tee box with good intentions of driving your ball straight down the fairway (the closely mowed area between the tee and the green). A slice is… well, it's frustrating and embarrassing at times. It happens a lot when you are learning the game, but it can happen to anyone—I've sliced a few balls in my day. It's when you hit the ball off the tee, but instead of going straight down the fairway, it curves wildly from left to right (for a right-handed player) and ultimately veers drastically to the right and away from your target.

Now, when you slice a ball, it can go anywhere as it swerves to the right. It can land in the woods, in a sand trap—anywhere that you don't want it. In recreational golf, rule #27 states that if you lose a ball hit from the tee, you can hit from the tee again or drop a ball two club-lengths back from where your ball exited the fairway. Either way, your score is one stroke from the tee, plus one penalty stroke for the lost ball. In other words, you are now hitting three—one stroke for the lost shot, plus the other two from the tee, thus the term, three off the tee.

This book, as the title suggests, is not a book about golf, but about targeting success in the workplace. So imagine for a moment that you have this thought: "Yikes. I just screwed up big time. I'm new and need to make the right impression. I'm not sure how to read all the politics. I have to fix this, but I'm not sure what I need to do. I may be at risk of losing my job or not being viewed as promotable. I may not get that new contract."

What usually happens is you start thinking of all the bad things that *could* happen to you instead of how you're going to fix the problem.

I've been in your shoes time and time again—the new employee or starting a new career, starting a new business or trying to figure out how to navigate all the potential hazards.

The best thing I can suggest when you find yourself in this situation is *golf*. Well, not golf exactly. I'm not telling you to actually go out and play a few rounds (even though that is sometimes the best therapy for me!). No, I'm talking about "golf" as a metaphor.

You see, I love golf, and I love it because, as in any game, you are always trying to improve. In golf, you're always working on your abilities and skills, but you also want to improve your score. And that's what makes it a great metaphor for business life. In the working world, you want to get better at what you do, but you also want to improve your skill sets and knowledge base, so you become a better employee or employer—the "score" part.

Golf is also a great metaphor for business because, in golf as in business, you are most often competing with yourself first, so you have to be honest with yourself, and you have to be open to change and growth. You must always accept that the scorecard tells all—whether you are making progress or not and where you need to focus.

Therefore, this is what I'm talking about when I say *golf* is a metaphor. Moreover, that's why I started the book with the idea of "three off the tee." When you make a bad play, in golf or in business, it's not the end of the world; it's just time to regroup, work a little harder, and get back on track. Sure, you may blow a few shots in the process, but you can't make forward progress all the time. However, when you run into trouble, and in fact even when you don't, the "three off the tee" rule helps you to recognize that you always have choices and decisions to make...and you have to make them. You analyze the best route to get yourself back on track, and you go for it.

Think about it. Our work life is full of choices: Do you answer that e-mail or leave it while you continue to work on the million-dollar proposal at hand? Do you decide to play devious, petty games by not telling a co-worker that he or she has a presentation to do (this actually happened to me, as you will read later)? Or, do you engage in a spirit of teamwork whereby you help your co-workers because you know that when individuals are winning, the team wins as well?

The other reason I like the golf metaphor is that, as both a hard-working, motivated person and an avid golfer, I find my work life is very much like a golf game.

Most of you are familiar with the idea of a "round" of golf. A "round" is actually eighteen holes, broken up into two groups of nine. That's the big picture, but like life, "big picture" stuff needs to be broken down into manageable parts and, in golf, the secret to playing well is to play each hole individually—just as you have to approach each problem that arises at work individually.

Now, each hole is approached in the same way. There are four main parts to a golf "hole": you start at the tee, hit down the fairway, get into the short game, which then puts you on the green (also known as the putting green). For each hole, you have to analyze the lay of the land and visualize your best shot. You need to set yourself up correctly and swing through. You have to keep your head, literally and figuratively, in the game, and you have to know what "par" is for the hole (*par* is the standard number of strokes in which a scratch golfer, a golfer with a zero handicap, would be expected to complete a hole or course). In addition, since you always allow for two putts, and holes can range from par three to par five, there's not a lot of room for error. This, however, is where golf gets interesting.

There are hazards built into the course—any bunker (a hollow or valley of some kind, usually filled with sand), water hazard (ocean, lake, pond, river, ditch, etc., usually marked with either white or red stakes or lines), or sloped bank that can hinder you from making par. Therefore, you strategize. You figure out what club needs to be used for the best advantage. You make the slope of the course work for you instead of against you. You constantly look for ways to improve—your grip, your stance, your alignment, and your set-up. You're always going for the cleanest shot so that you make par or under.

You repeatedly practice all of the tough shots to master them. Like most golfers, I always work hard to improve my game. I record *everything* on my scorecard, so I can easily highlight my strengths and weaknesses. In addition to my score, I record my drive length, whether I make the fairway, if I am on the green in regulation (playing your ball onto the green in the prescribed number of strokes as determined by par or simply par for the hole, less two strokes for putting), and the number of putts I take to sink the ball. There are days when I wonder what I am doing on the course, and then there are other days when I can do no wrong. I *love* the days when I hit awesome pro-like shots—it's those shots that keep me coming back, no matter how few and far between they may be!

The golf-as-work metaphor, then, works like this: You play every day as if it's a new day. You approach your day by strategizing how to get the maximum impact for that day (the best shot, as it were). You need to set yourself up right; you definitely need to keep your head in the game, and you need to keep accurate score of how you are performing, so that you can plan for continuous improvement, moving forward toward your ultimate goal. This is the process of improvement—you work smart, you practice, you plan, you lower your score, and you succeed.

The analogies I could make to golf are endless—and you're going to hear about them throughout the book. That being said, *3 Off the Tee: Targeting Success* isn't just a golf book. It's your personal challenge to improve and take a good hard look at what is important in your work life. By using healthy competition, taking responsibility for what is good and bad in your life, planning for improvement, and taking hazards out of play, you can reinvent your world.

Know that by reading this book, you already recognize the value of improving. You are working to improve yourself and make yourself invaluable to your company. As you start or progress in your journey in the work world, think about having a personal scorecard where you can record how you are doing on a regular basis. Succeeding in work, and in life, is so much easier when you do just this one step because, with that scorecard, you can focus on what is important to your goals, deal with day-to-day obstacles, and make good decisions.

What I hope you get out of this book is some inspiration and direction. It's not intended to tell you how to do your job better. I don't talk about how to write goals, organize your desk, or about doing your job—even though that's important—it's more about your work attitude, the work attitude you need to become successful. A solid work attitude comes from a positive mind, a good work ethic, and a willingness to learn. Attitude shows in how you carry yourself through your day, how you handle problems, and how you inspire yourself to work smarter.

What it all comes down to is that, when you have direction, you can grab hold of challenge, brainstorm, come up with ideas and solutions, put a plan in place, and chase down results. That's what I hope you gain from *3 Off the Tee: Targeting Success.*

As you read, think of the following three sentences as your mantra:

- o I thrive on making things happen, and once I'm on board, the challenge is mine.

- o I am not deterred when I make a bad play; I just regroup and keep on going.

- o Ultimately, I know that a bad play simply means that I still have some work to do.

Working to the best of your ability is not about being perfect by any means. However, by adding a jolt of self-awareness, infused with some real-life course management, you can get your life into play.

So tee up and let's get going!

Targeting Success is the first of a series of motivational self-improvement books to be published under the *3 Off the Tee* brand.

The Front Nine
Self-Perception & Self-Direction

Trust your swing

The 1st Hole - Self-assess and shift your attitude
The 2nd Hole - Learn to improve
The 3rd Hole - Break down barriers
The 4th Hole - Focus on making decisions
The 5th Hole - Upgrade your confidence
The 6th Hole - Accept challenge
The 7th Hole - Relationship equity part one:
    Recognize positive influence
The 8th Hole - Relationship equity part two:
    Communicate fairly
The 9th Hole - Utilize your strengths

In school, we had teachers and professors guiding us. They told us when to turn in our homework and what to study for on the tests; they taught us the basics. They were our mentors, feeding our brains, and our referees, keeping us in check, in

---

control, and on track for the most part. For those of you who went through the school system from 1970 onward, you heard more and more about self-esteem and its importance to your personal development. There was an attempt to build students up through recognition of achievements, both in the class and through extracurricular activity.

Today, though, amazingly enough, schools discourage the idea of "winners" and "losers"—in other words, to build your self-esteem, they took competition out of the game. I find this disheartening and counterproductive. You have to learn how to strategize in order to win; and then, when you do win, you feel great about it. Equally important is learning how to be a good sport when you lose. You can't win all the time, so you regroup, learn from it, and get ready for the next game. If you are reading this book, it's because you want to be better—to make yourself more promotable as an employee or more effective as an employer. You're probably competitive by nature, and that's a strong and healthy start.

It has been my experience as an employer that my new employees, while they come to me fresh from completing their training programs with college or university degrees and are skilled in their field to a greater or lesser extent, don't know how to play the corporate game. They don't yet know how to be a stellar employee, the kind that upper management "keeps their eye on" because they're looking to promote that person.

The corporate game is competitive—really competitive. There are winners and losers every day, and you need to know what the winners know. It's not enough just to survive; you need to know how to break through and thrive in the business world.

To stand out in such a highly competitive environment, you need to have the right attitude about yourself. You need to develop a smart work ethic—one of discipline, integrity, and moral fiber. Those who work all the extra hours or overtime are not always considered the "best" employees. It's the people who work "smarter," not necessarily "harder," that win and keep winning the corporate golf game.

And is it ever a game, one of the most intense, most strategized games there is—so, let's look at how to approach this game by getting you set up and aligned so that you are aimed properly at your intended target. That's what these first nine "holes" are all about—your perception of yourself, how you handle yourself in intense situations, all those things for which you have "self-" as a prefix, and if done right, those things that can give you some of the best self-esteem on the planet!

How you see yourself develops through a combination of attitude changes based on how you perceive your behavior and how you feel others respond to that behavior. If you observe that responses to your behavior are favorable, you will feel liked, respected, and loved, which directly influences your attitude. Such positive reinforcement builds self-esteem and breeds confidence.

In a way, you're not unlike a new golfer. He or she may begin by swinging twenty or thirty times before even making contact with the ball. It takes time, practice, and determination to get to the point where you trust your swing. When you do, it will be because you have upgraded your skill sets. You will be able to focus, as you will have developed control through muscle memory. Knowing that you can make solid contact with the ball gives you confidence and brings you to a new level where you can further hone your skills and improve your score through practice, accuracy, and course management.

First things first though. The first nine holes in this round of work-life improvement are all about focusing on building a positive self-perception. You see, it's not enough to be smart. You were no doubt hired because you have the right credentials or experience, or both. To really excel and become successful, however, you need to know how to build yourself up and push yourself beyond the ordinary.

You have to trust your swing, and to do that, you have to be able to trust yourself.

Swing Thoughts:

Set goals and objectives
for self-improvement.

Develop a solid action plan and
be accountable and unbiased.

Evaluate and modify your plan
regularly and stay the course.

Trust Your Swing

The 1ˢᵗ Hole - Self-assess and shift your attitude

Scream out…"I AM AMAZING!"

(Hey, that was easy…now let's work on making you believe it!)

Okay, just like in any game, you have to "come out to play" if you intend to win. Golf is no different, and neither is the workplace. When you address the ball, when you walk to your desk, do so with confidence and purpose. You don't want your opponents or team to think that you don't know what you're doing or that you don't have the direction and desire to be a contender.

Think about it. If you come to work with your shoulders drooping, and you think, "I hate my life," or "I hate being here," what do you think others are going to think of you? For that matter, what do *you* think of you? After all, it is what *you* think that matters.

For example, a good friend of mine recently referred to me as fearless. She nonchalantly threw it out there in a conversation, as if it was just common knowledge. My ears perked up and my tail started wagging. I thought, "Wow!"

Well, let me tell you, I totally did not see that coming, and although I don't know if I can live up to it, I liked it!

I was told that I am fearless because I am always ready to jump in with both feet and try new things, apparently things that others find too challenging or perhaps risky. I think I may appear fearless because I live by the saying, "Never let them see you sweat." Either way, I was fearlessly flattered and perhaps a little more fearless because of this positive recognition.

In all aspects of my life, I endeavor to be direct, professional, honest, composed, and confident. I do a good job—I like who I am. A positive self-perception is the basis for how I feel about myself but there is so much more to it.

Build your self-perception.

Self-perception is not only how you see yourself, it's an extremely powerful personal resource. You can self-assess, shift your attitude, and change in order to unveil a new and improved version of yourself—all within the course of a few seconds. Try this simple exercise. Decide to be confident and charming and smack a huge Cheshire cat smile across your face. No matter what mood you are in, just decide for this one moment that you are happy...awesome.

Now, do the opposite. Decide that you are going to be miserable and pissed off about everything. See—you are the person in control of how you feel, and you are most certainly in control of your attitude.

Here is the million-dollar question though—how do you see yourself? Do you think of yourself as in charge, even fearless? Or, do you think of yourself as someone who does not know much, so you stay back, not wanting anyone to know that you really don't have much to offer?

Well, hey, listen up. Do you think you would have been hired in the first place if you didn't have much to offer? Someone saw potential. So now, it is up to you to prove them right. Show them that you are confident of your abilities and that you came out to play...and win!

How you see yourself defines how you see yourself in the world—your demeanor, your attitude, and how you expect others to respond to you. It permeates your physical, visual, and verbal self, as well as how you approach and tackle life. Therefore, if there are times in your life when you feel some of your personality traits are restricting your growth, you better dial them back, and then punch up those traits you want to surface.

Don't give your opponents the chance to take the upper hand whether in a game of golf or at work. You don't want other golfers in your foursome to think of you as being weak. Not because they can do anything overt with that information, but because when they think of you as weak, they gain a sense of power.

In evaluating your self-perception, you have to be brutally honest and willing to acknowledge both your strengths and your weaknesses. You have to persuade yourself that you have what it takes and then run with it. Build up your self-esteem, purge negative, self-diminishing habits, and believe that you are amazing! Okay, that may be a feat easier said than done, but then again, maybe not. Think about how easy it was to decide you were confident and happy. You can decide that you are good enough and know that you have what it takes to excel!

Learn to lust after life.

I love to watch passionate people in action. They exude charisma and warmth, and they lust after life. They have an indisputable attraction—their insatiable passion for living life to the fullest and their desire to make things happen. They have self-directed purpose and tend not to get dragged down by self-doubt or distraction.

It is that undying determination, extra exertion or effort, or different outlook or approach they have that intrigues us. We are drawn to them, wanting to feel, dream, and understand as they do.

The drive and desire—and yes, we all have it—comes from inside. It starts with believing in yourself and knowing that you are amazing and finishes with success—as you define it.

Take a good hard look in the mirror and self-assess. Describe how you see yourself with respect to your physical, visual, verbal self, your approach, and how you think others see you. Then think about how you want to be seen.

The Physical You:

It is a well-known fact that you can achieve immense confidence from being physically fit, healthy, and strong. You walk taller, are lighter on your feet, and are ready for anything, because you are confident that you can hold your own.

When you work out, you feel better physically, you feel better about yourself, and everything in everyday life starts to look better and feel more manageable. Whenever someone is having a difficult time in life, getting back to the basics of feeling good inside is the best place to start rebuilding.

Take a minute to consider your weight, your physical fitness level, as well as how you look, both dressed and naked. Do you appear healthy? Do you look younger or older than your age?

The Visual You:

Next, how do you rank visually? This is a bit of a spillover from the physical you, but it's intended to be more about your body language—the "you" that is defined by your movements, gestures, expressions, and tone.

Do you walk with a confident stride? Are you visually animated and vibrant? Do you possess an innate talent for attracting and holding attention when you engage in conversation? Is the tone of your voice forceful and melodic, rendering you alive and interesting?

The Verbal You:

Now, orally, what is the meaning others perceive when they digest the words that are trickling out of your mouth? Do you come across as being candid and authentic? Do you actually care about the message you are sending out?

Do others observe that you are alert, smart, interested, and involved? Do they believe in what you are talking about and feel that you have something important to say?

Your Approach:

Finally, think about how you approach and tackle life. Are you a straight shooter, even-tempered, and dependable? Do you adapt easily to any situation, take charge, and get results? Are you trustworthy and sincere, and generally good to have around?

Honest self-assessment and evaluation can lead to positive growth through shifting attitudes.

Take an honest look at yourself and describe what you see. List the characteristics and attributes that define who you are. Do you believe that you are amazing, talented, charismatic, or successful? Make a list of personal traits that are important to you, and then answer this very important question: Do you like and respect yourself?

Now evaluate the physical, visual, and verbal you, and draft a game plan for improvement. Remember that it is important to live your life to the fullest, recognize opportunities, and take control of how you live your life so that you do not let life happen to you.

Living your life to the fullest begins with having an insatiable zest for life and being passionate about your dreams and expectations.

We all carry around a self-image that keeps us in check in everyday life, and that self-image comes to work with us every day. We also have a confident and free-spirited inner self that is daring and perfect—in our own minds, of course. But think of how setting your inner-self free may in fact set you free, leaving you more open to put yourself out there and really start living.

Why not shift some of your inner power and strength into gear and rev up some positive attitude? With a positive attitude of "I can" instead of "I'll try," you will find that you can take some calculated risks at your own pace and, therefore, stretch. You can build yourself up knowing that change, newness, and challenge breed confidence and excitement. You can be amazing!

So I ask you, why hold back? What good could that possibly do?

We, as human beings, enjoy freedom of choice. Your attitude is your choice!

Trust Your Swing

The 2nd Hole - **Learn to improve**

You can teach yourself how to improve.

In golf, you address the ball. This means that you are in position and prepared to hit. At this point, your main concern is whether you are properly aimed at your intended target and whether you are ready to take your shot.

In order to be mentally prepared for your swing, you run through a shot planner or pre-swing routine. There are three basic considerations to keep in mind: am I properly set up, am I properly aligned, and is my ball in the correct position? You need to take a minute to visualize the shot from behind the ball and perhaps even choose an intermediate spot in front of the ball, in line with your primary target, to use as an alignment aid.

This is a learned process. You started out with limited knowledge and experience, but then you worked hard and practiced until you developed your shot plan, your swing, muscle memory, and abilities.

As a result, you are able to visualize your shot; you can walk up to the tee with confidence. You have the attitude of a winner, and everyone can sense it. You have taken the motto "learn to improve" to heart.

With most everything in golf, and in life, you have to admit when you don't know enough or have the right skills to hit your target. Then you can identify what you need to know and work hard to get there. When you adopt this type of attitude, you become unstoppable.

People learn when they are ready to learn. Be ready to learn, accept challenge, and take on the world.

We compete in life every day. We thrive on and desire attention, recognition, opportunity for advancement, and security. We strive to become more fit in our minds through self-improvement, growth, and maturity. We are most effective at learning, though, when we have made up our minds to learn, when we have the desire to learn, and have committed our efforts.

Here is an interesting concept. Think of everyone as having untapped, unexploited potential. It is always there no matter where your life has taken you, what you have already accomplished, and whether you are young or old. Think about everyone as having potential that is on reserve just waiting for them to say, "I'm ready."

If you can accept this way of thinking, you will always be ready to learn, knowing that your potential is an infinite, renewable resource.

This is true for your life at work as much as it is in your life outside of work. One of the most amazing things to realize is that, if you do not like an aspect of your life, you have the potential and ability to change it.

Take a good hard look at yourself and try to distinguish what your weakest personality link is. What part of your demeanor or thought process needs to be improved so that you are not holding yourself back from achieving your goals?

For example, say that overly aggressive, obnoxious people intimidate you. Most of us do feel some sort of anxiety when exposed to this type of in-your-face behavior. The point here is to learn to push past your feeling of intimidation so that you are in control rather than upset and distracted. Think back to a time when some annoying individual out-and-out pissed you off and you were caught dead in your tracks. In a state of shock, you stood speechless and furious. They cockily exited leaving you to rethink and relive your unfortunate meeting over and over again. From that point on, you probably assured yourself that the next time you were in such a situation, you would be ready with a witty and brilliant reply, thus rendering your opponent dumbfounded and diminished.

Well, perhaps in a perfect world, your perfect self would be ready to take care of any situation with impeccable grace and ease. In fact, your perfect inner self would also be ready with the right speech, the tactful diversion in an embarrassing moment, or the perfectly executed pearl of wisdom that even a disgruntled co-worker would buy.

Unfortunately, though, we do not live in a perfect world, and rethinking and reliving uncomfortable situations won't change a thing. What you can do, however, is work toward unleashing some of your perfect inner self so that you learn to improve by asserting yourself with confidence.

Okay, so what if I want a mulligan (a "do-over")?

Here's how it works. A situation arises and you think, feel, and react. You cringe. You hate when you act like this. Perhaps you let someone take credit for your hard work, or you didn't speak up because you felt intimidated.

Here's what you do: Think about a workplace situation where you may feel intimidated or restricted in some way. What will it take for you to get past such feelings? Appraise where you see yourself fitting in, what personality traits support that role, and what you need to do to get there.

Take time to detail and analyze various situations that you find uncomfortable in the workplace and pay attention to your reaction in each case. Then, look past your reaction and try to identify its trigger. What was your thought process? Did the hair rise on the back of your neck? If so, when? How did you react? Was your response too meek or too aggressive?

Here's a great example of what I am talking about. Quite a few years back I had an employee that worked in reception. She was punctual, bright, and an absolute delight to be around. The problem was that she was not viewed as being promotable. When certain senior management would ask a simple question such as how her day was going, she would provide a funny story from her personal life or perhaps offer a little too much information—comments more suitable for after work with friends. Usually after the fact, she would feel embarrassed by her comments, regretting them. She was fun and vivacious, but not promotable.

One day I asked her if she was happy in her position with the company. She wasn't. She wanted to advance and had been taking college business courses at night in hopes of moving into accounting or marketing. I told her that I noticed that quite often when her superiors asked her direct questions, she often appeared uncomfortable, and I questioned whether she felt out of control during those instances.

She immediately understood what I was talking about. She did feel anxious and nervous when talking to superiors, and then she would find herself blurting out a silly, awkward response without thinking. Her temperature would rise and a feverish sweat would spread across her face.

She needed to take this new knowledge and put it into play. She rehearsed some more suitable responses in front of the mirror at night until she was no longer anxious and intimidated in these situations. She became collected and more professional in her approach, and a couple of months later when an opening became available in the office, she got the promotion.

Work consists of a series of similar situations repeating again and again, flavored by the various reactions of the different people involved each time. That being said, when a similar situation arises, you can consciously be aware and ready to alter your response and deal with the aftermath. If you think about the workplace this way, you can see that it is an excellent stage for learning to assert yourself in familiar surroundings. Practice makes perfect!

As you work your way along this process, you will find that upward progression will result even if you fumble through, because, when you forge ahead, you create new patterns of behavior. New, more positive behavior is generally more comfortable, and so there is a tendency to keep moving forward and never look back. Every time you change your game, you gain more control over your own reaction and the situation.

Your mind can be as open as you let your world be, and your world can be as open as you let your mind be.

Focus inwardly on self-imposed shortcomings long enough to establish your weakest personality link. Create a pre-swing thought or drill whereby you can act through situations that you find uncomfortable or restrictive. Strengthen your response and behavior and refocus on being the best that you can be. This is your mullie (mulligan or do-over). Take advantage of it and learn to improve.

Remember that it's a big world out there and you can do whatever you choose. Unleash your potential and come out swinging!

To desire to change one's past means there is a desire to change oneself. To desire to change oneself, one must learn to change.

Trust Your Swing

The 3rd Hole - **Break down barriers**

Don't build roadblocks out of assumptions.

It is amazing to see young kids at the driving range. They grab a club, whirl it around, balance it upright on the tip of their finger like a basketball, and then take a swing that seems effortless and natural. I have yet to see a new adult golfer display such confidence and ease. As adults, many of us have lost a lot of our physical intuitiveness. We are afraid of making fools of ourselves, and we have a difficult time accepting that we aren't instantly good at whatever we try.

Golfing requires a surprising amount of strength and stamina. You need to attack the hole. This is where the old saying, "It can't go in if it can't get there," comes into play. You have to strike with precision to make accurate contact with the ball and you have to go for the shot aggressively. It is better to be just past your target than fall short of it.

Many recreational golfers adopt a "swing lightly" mentality, meaning they do not put a lot of "umpf" into the ball. They do so because they have found that they can hit the ball squarely more frequently if they do not swing through with as much club-head speed. Therefore, they simply lose the will to be aggressive and progressive in honing their physical skills. They lose their edge and choose to play it safe rather than pushing past their barrier in order to become a better golfer.

I am sure you can see where this one is going. Since our first nine holes are about "self"—self-improvement, self-esteem, and all those things—it is important to be aggressive about building your "self" up.

Here are some typical "swing lightly" thoughts:

- o Do you tell yourself that you aren't good enough, smart enough, or strong enough?

- o Do you fill in the blanks with assumptions and turn yourself into an emotional mess?

- o Are you obsessed with every little detail about yourself?

If so, you are setting up roadblocks that you need to aggressively knock down.

Let me give you some specific work examples:

The Complacent, "Swing Lightly," Thought Process:

Hmmm...
I think they will overlook me for the promotion.
Maybe my credentials were not good enough,
maybe my review was not positive,
or maybe I am too nervous.
Maybe I don't want the promotion after all.

What? Have you done this? Have you talked yourself right out of something for no real reason?

Don't start second-guessing yourself. It is self-defeating and deflating. And, hey, if you are going to start filling in the blanks with assumptions—assume the positive!

The Aggressive, "Barrier-breaking" Thought Process:

Hmmm...
I am excited about this possibility
of promotion.
They must be taking a good
look at my credentials,

and I know that my performance
reviews have been great.
I feel confident.
I have a lot to offer and I am
up for the challenge.

It is so important to stick to the facts and not assume. Strip out emotion and watch how much easier it is to be objective and get to the root of things. Have you ever really sat and thought about how negative thoughts manage to creep into your mind? Have you ever really thought about why you let it happen in the first place?

Rewrite your mental vocabulary.

People who aggressively break down their barriers to success are also known for being mentally tough. Now I don't have to go into detail about how golf is a game of mental toughness—most games are, and work is no different. The point is that many people enter the workforce with similar skill sets and know the technical aspects of the job, but those with mental toughness last and climb the ladder to success.

One of the best ways to be mentally tough is to think tough—not in an evil way, but in the best, most positive way possible.

Here is an example of what I mean.

Remove the word "hopefully" from your vocabulary.

I once worked for a rather brilliant man who used this strategy. We would sit around the boardroom table at 7:00 a.m. (so as not interfere with the official workday that started promptly at 8:00 a.m.) and discuss what wins as well as what improvements had taken place in each facet of the business.

His overall plan for the company was comprised of the combination of business plans, generated by each of his trusted managers. This meant we all had to have solid working plans to generate more business; we had to find new ways to make production more efficient, so we would be more competitive, work towards expanding our market-share, and generate a stronger bottom line.

My boss also had another ironclad rule. The word "hopefully" was stricken from our vocabulary. It was a smart rule. "Hopefully" was like making excuses up front and setting the stage for failure.

It worked. The company thrived.

Make your plan and make it work by whatever means it takes, but never, never, ever say that "hopefully" something might happen.

Remove "I could haves" from your vocabulary.

I like to be creative, come up with different ideas, and run with them. I involve others if I need help or if a team effort is required. Mostly, though, if my independent effort is all that is required—I go for it!

When I hear people say, "I could have" while expressing regret for missed opportunities, my immediate response is, "Yeah, you could have, but you didn't." I am sorry, but this is black and white to me. If there is something that you want to do, do it. Don't talk about it! Don't hesitate. If you need upper-level permission, then write a proposal and get on it. Your "can do" attitude is going to go a lot further than a "could have" mentality.

There are simple great words to live by: "I am," "I can," "I will"...

Removing the words "hopefully" and "I could have" from your vocabulary, however, is not enough to be mentally tough. You need to replace them with "look at what I am doing" or "look at what I can do" and then set the world on fire! These powerful yet simple words are often referred to as "affirmations." They are short, positive statements and thoughts in the present tense, statements like, "I do great work," "I thrive at my job," and then after the fact, you might say something like, "I did a great job!" In other words,

I am asking you to build a winning vocabulary that will encourage direction and success. The "toughest" part of this type of thinking, however, is that you have to continue to think those positive thoughts even when things aren't going so well. By keeping your mental toughness going, you will break down barriers all over the place—not just within the work environment.

You have had many successes, and you have earned the right to be respected.

Mental toughness means you have to pay attention to all of your thoughts. Here is a barrier-breaking trick that I call "er-rant-ication." It is, basically, the eradication of rants or complaints in your day-to-day work life. Think of how an errant golf ball can cost you a stroke in golf; a ranting mentality can cost you opportunities in your work life.

Here is what you do. For one full day, whenever a negative thought or complaint comes to mind, write it down. Write down even the most minor things, and try to be totally honest and aware of what you are thinking. At the end of the day, look at how many times you felt like complaining. Look at whether any of your complaints were valid.

Now, this is the most important part—this is the part where you aggressively swing at the ball as opposed to just playing it safe—deal with valid complaints and eradicate the rest so that they no longer pile up and create barriers for you.

If there is something you want to do, but a barrier you have built is holding you back, you need to work toward taking it down. Focus on the many successes that you have had in your life and repeatedly relive that feeling of success. The more you build yourself up, the more you will develop a positive forward approach. Your winning vocabulary will result in winning habits.

Self-affirm—build yourself up with honest and genuine praise.

o Make a list of your feelings and identify them as being either negative or positive.

o Tackle your negative feelings and work on replacing them with positive ones.

Keep adding to the positive feelings list and write down things that mean something to you. In golf, you use a swing thought. A saying, tune, or beat that gets you focused and ready to make your shot.

I like the following poem that I wrote a few years ago. To me it says, I am strong, smart, and in charge!

The color is red…
fury, strength.
I will wear it with fury
and take back all that is mine.

The sensation is willful…
powerful and wondrous.
I will entertain only the positive
and reclaim my mind.

I will drink in my world.
I will find it intoxicating.
I will share my life's lust with all who dare to fly.
I will open my heart and learn to trust again.

If I cannot climb the wall, I will break it down.

Trust Your Swing

The 4th Hole - **Focus on making decisions**

Sometimes the easiest solution is just to get it done.

No matter how much you plan or how positively you think, life is going to catch you off guard from time to time, and whether on the golf course or in the workplace, you're going to have to make some decisions and deal.

On the golf course, whenever you have an errant shot—a shot that leaves you in long grass, under a tree, in loose and tangled brush, or in the water—you will need a recovery shot to get your ball back into play. In essence, your recovery shot should allow you to recover. Therefore, your recovery shot needs to be set up so that you have a good lie and are in position to make your next shot. One wasted shot is enough. By being observant and proactive, you can take hold of any situation, deal with it, and stay on course.

Work is no different. You have a presentation due and you require help from a co-worker who is supposed to be preparing schedules or diagrams for you. Don't leave things until the last minute and then panic or, even worse, fail to do your presentation altogether. No one will remember that someone may have let you down. They, however, will remember that you weren't ready.

No matter what the situation (and I am sure you can think of thousands of them,) you have two choices—you either can leave things to chance and complain about them, or you can deal with them. It's always best to take ownership and get results.

Life has its challenges. That is reality.

Sometimes you are forced to deal with stuff that is not so pleasant. This is a huge stumbling point for many people. They are uncomfortable with what they know has to happen, so they tend to agonize and internalize their problems instead of dealing with them. Therefore, they relive uncomfortable situations and struggle through life. They never get to the bottom of things.

Pack away disappointment, anger, and regret. Just deal with stuff and be finished with it. Remember the lesson, share the lesson, but do not continue to relive the angst and drag related parties through the mess again and again. It is over! Do not let the negative steal your zest for life. Get rid of excuses.

If it's over, leave it in the past!

The trick is really to deal with issues. I mean, get to the bottom of whatever is causing you grief. If you try to fool yourself and say that you have dealt with a problem when you haven't, trust me, it will rear its ugly head repeatedly until you finally, and for the last time, deal with it.

By dealing with stuff in a timely basis, you reduce your exposure to failure. A proactive approach minimizes the risk of hazards and sets you up to have the best game of your life. Success in the workplace is built around being consistent, reliable, and ready.

You even have to deal with the good stuff.

There are always opportunities out there—the good stuff, the stuff you want to pull in from the fringe and make reality. You can only do this if you are ready. So take care of business and never leave anything to chance, especially those things that are important to you.

Every day, good and bad things happen that require your attention. You can deal with it now or deal with it later but, either way, you will have to deal with it, so you may as well just do it now. Of course, right now you are thinking...what? Do I have to deal with good stuff, too? Well, yes, and the procrastinators among you best pay attention.

Maybe you have found your dream house but wonder how you can afford it, or you have been offered an amazing career opportunity, but you will have to uproot and move your family. Day-to-day opportunities are laced with challenges that need to be headed off and dealt with so that you can move ahead.

What I am really getting at here is that things don't just happen. You make them happen by taking hold of situations, dealing with aspects that need resolution, deciphering what information is required to make a decision, and then making the decision.

Sometimes you just have to believe.

The number one rule is, *know that what goes around, comes around*. At work, this means that, when someone has done something to you that had a negative impact on your life and it's out of your control, let it go. Deal with it by letting it go and moving on. Believe that, at some point, that person's wrongdoing, or perhaps failure to do what he or she should have, will come back and bite him or her in the ass!

Quite often, people blow a lot of time, energy, and effort trying to figure out why things turned out wrong or, moreover, how to get even. It is not important in the grand scheme of things and is a total waste of your time. For example, if you have a colleague who continually does not pull his or her weight, do not let that colleague drag you down. Take the initiative to work around his or her inabilities or resistance and make headway independent of him or her. You did not hire this person, so you are not in the position to reprimand him or her; so, since this situation is out of your control, you deal with it by coming up with an alternate solution.

Once you accept this as fact, it is usually easier to move on and redirect your attention to what is important for you.

Your initiative and stick-to-itiveness will make you stronger and more confident of your abilities, and others will recognize your achievements, as well as the lack of assistance you received from your colleague.

Do not waste time trying to figure everything out. It's not a work requirement.

Some people will do whatever it takes to get out of dealing with stuff. They are happy to live a counterfeit existence, fantasizing to escape from everyday difficulties. They imagine their way out of bad situations as though in a state of "transcendental meditation," blocking in order to get through the tough stuff.

Remember that escapism is an illusion, and it is fleeting at best. Then you are back at the bottom trying to climb up again.

Sometimes the hardest thing to do is to confront something you don't want to. We make that horrible thing that we know we have to deal with really complex—because, when it's complex, we can justify to ourselves why we didn't deal with it.

That's not how to get things done. If the idea of work is to "work"—to get the job done—then you just have to take a deep breath and figure it out. Here are some things that have helped me just deal with stuff:

o Record your thoughts and feelings in a journal. Yes, I know. That's something people do in their personal lives. However, it works well in your work life as well. Really, think about how much time you spend at work. And, yes, writing in a journal is time consuming, but it's worth it. Why? Because, quite often, we talk ourselves out of things without even realizing it. We shrug off things that are important to us by thinking, "I'm too busy for that right now," "I'm not ready," or "I don't have enough education," without really thinking things through. We do it all of the time. We haphazardly and unknowingly shut our thoughts and concerns down. Start by being aware of when you start to shut down or second-guess yourself. Write the details down. I guarantee that you will surprise yourself, and you will quickly start to see patterns forming.

o When you have a situation that you don't want to deal with, write down all the things that would have to happen in order to fix that situation. Figure out the one thing on the list that is easy for you to do (it doesn't have to be the most important thing, just the easiest to deal with) and do it. Sometimes starting is the hardest part. Start the process and watch how all the other things you need to deal with fall into place.

o If it is a big situation, you may not have to deal with it all on your own. Figure out which part you must deal with, and then make a list of potential teammates. Clear that list with your boss, if you need to, and then get all those people involved. Have them each make a list of things they need to do to deal with the situation, tell them to start with the one that is easiest for them, and then watch as your joint efforts get the results you want—a done deal!

Dealing with stuff is a process that can be continually perfected and improved. It is a winning strategy, and of the utmost importance when trying to progress in the workplace.

Errant shot or not—know that you have a recovery shot in your bag! Deal with stuff, make decisions, and move forward!

Trust Your Swing

The 5th Hole -
Upgrade your confidence

There is confidence convergence when mental prowess and business aptitude mesh.

Confidence in yourself and your ability to do your job is crucial to workplace success.

Many different components go into building one's confidence. It is having done the time and knowing that you have what it takes to get the job done. As in golf, it is being able to focus, visualizing the shot, and having the guts to go for it. It is having an underlying sense of ability that enables you to set aside self-deprecating thoughts and refocus on the big picture.

I am certain that you've heard of something being a *fluke* before, but did you realize that a hole-in-one is never a fluke? In golf, a fluke occurs when you make an unexpected shot. A hole-in-one cannot possibly be a fluke because it is exactly what you were aiming for! The perfect shot! If you have been working hard, honing your skills, checking and rechecking your grip, stance, and swing, then your hole-in-one is your reward. And believe me, a hole-in-one, or more commonly any great shot, gives you a ton of confidence in your game.

Since this is a book about developing the right attitude to be successful in the workplace, what better attitude to have than that of confidence?

There are actually two basic sources of confidence. The first is the homegrown type, which develops through the repetitious support of parents and inspirational teachers, coaches, and mentors. They help you see what is good about yourself, and by doing so, you build confidence in your abilities.

The second source of confidence develops through the success of overcoming obstacles. This starts in your early life, but it is an ongoing deal. In the workplace, the whole concept of "thinking outside the box" comes to mind. Sometimes a new direction or idea is required, and there is no historical data or experiences from which to pull past solutions. This is when persistence and ingenuity are required to overcome the obstacles at hand. When you can make this happen, you build confidence from your own doing. You realize that you may not be able to count on others or the past, but you can count on yourself.

Either way, you figure it out, and real confidence stays with you forever—and this is how it adds up to workplace success: Others inherently recognize and feel your confidence when they are in your presence, and it shows in everything you do. When you have confidence, people come to you to get help, and they tend to respect you more. People who truly have confidence in their ability to do their jobs well generally enjoy a healthy sense of job satisfaction and feel happier about themselves.

Sometimes it is all in your head.

Confidence starts in your head. It is the center of how we feel about what we have achieved in our lives. It is commonly referred to as being critical to achieving success when we look at action-oriented sports. It is part of the mental preparation needed to help an athlete excel in his or her field. It is deemed an integral focus when trying to develop a competitive edge.

That being said, you can mentally exercise and build your confidence prowess! It is actually very simple:

1) Relive your successes, conquests, and accomplishments. Create a list for easy reference. We sometimes overlook and take our "wins" for granted, but our repeated wins evolve into winning habits, making it easier to push for more.

2) Take what you want to accomplish next and visualize the outcome that you desire—every detail—with clarity and conviction. This is like visualizing the shot in golf. You analyze everything—the landscape of the hole, the hazards, the lie—so that you are confident and able to commit to the shot.

3) Play it forward. Go for it and continually add new successes to your list.

4) Celebrate the wins.

When mental confidence is coupled with physical confidence there is magic.

Even though confidence starts in your head, it carries through in how you present yourself physically. You do not have to be drop-dead gorgeous to be physically confident. It is more about how you carry yourself. It is in the way you dress, the care with which you groom yourself, your fitness level, a nice physique, a friendly appearance, and a comfortable manner. All of these little things can add to your sense of confidence. And your physical confidence is noticed as much as your mental confidence. It is in visual perception where you usually generate the first set of stimuli to catch others' attention in a social situation.

It is in the way you sound when you talk. How your voice sounds and your way of moving play important roles. A deep booming voice, raspy fun-loving voice, or sweet and gentle voice, all command a different appeal for different people. When you walk lightly with poise and control or walk firmly with a carefree gate, you create an audible dimension, which contributes to your overall appeal.

It is even about your personal scent, whether natural or artificial. For instance, I find some scents unbearable as I suffer from allergies. That being said, there may be something to rethinking your perfume or cologne selection.

Everyone admires attractive people, and it's a fact that good looks will take a person a long way in our society. However, if those good looks are not backed up by mental confidence and competence, then you're just not in the game.

You need the whole package. Attitude about yourself and about your work is undoubtedly the most important attribute to consider here.

Your attitude comes from inside. When you are able to relax and let your true personality shine through, you come across as confident and interesting. You appear to like, respect, and believe in yourself. When that happens, people like being around you. They like working with you, and they trust your competence level. They know that you will make certain that things are done right.

Your appearance, attitude, and confidence define you as a person.

A professional, well-dressed golfer, like a businessperson, gives the impression that he thinks that the golf course and/or workplace and the people there are important.

Trust Your Swing

The 6th Hole -
Accept challenge

Bring it on!

It is not enough to accept the challenge to be willing to learn and improve. You need to take what you have learned and put it into play. You have to step up and into the challenge. Step outside of your comfort zone and be ready and willing to accept new challenges.

Golf offers a multilevel and seemingly limitless source of personal challenges. First, you are playing against the course, and there is a wide variety of course difficulty as defined by par for the course, the overall length, and the slope (a rating of the relative playing difficulty of a course for players who are not scratch golfers). Second, you are playing against yourself by trying to reduce your overall score and handicap (the average difference between a series of a player's scores and a set standard). Third, you can compete against others based on your total score for 18 holes (stroke play) or on a hole-by-hole basis (match play), where you compete with another player or team. You can also play level (straight up) or off handicap. I think you get the idea, right?

Well, work is no different. And the more challenges you accept, the more you learn and the more you become willing to take on new challenges.

Here is what I mean. Last year, when my weight was creeping up, I threw out a little competitive challenge to a bunch of my friends. Golf season was coming, and we were all complaining about gaining weight over the winter. This is not a major breakthrough, but hey, it worked for us.

This is the challenge I e-mailed out:

Preseason Tune-up!

Here it is!
Sweet and simple.
Lose some weight and perhaps make
some cash.
It all comes down to...how competitive are you?

Here's how it works.

———

*First, you commit to lose ten pounds.
Then, you pay $500.00 into a weight-loss fund.
For every pound you lose...
you earn back $50.00.*

*If you lose the full ten pounds it costs
you nothing BUTT...(pun intended)
you will have lost ten pounds.
At the end of the program, if you have
lost your ten pounds you will also
get to split the balance of the cash not
earned back by your opponents,
who, for whatever reason, didn't
lose the whole ten pounds.*

E-mail me to join...

*Every day text or e-mail your weight to me.
Your weight loss program starts today...
and final weigh-in is Friday, May 16th.*

Let's see what kind of a loser you really are!

Everyone who took the challenge succeeded. They all lost ten or more pounds. For some, the competition alone was enough; they kept track of everyone's weight loss, and it kept them focused. Others were motivated by the fact that their competitors were planning on how they would spend their winnings, and there was no way they would be the one paying out for that to happen.

I had the least amount of weight to lose and, surprisingly, lost the last half pound by the morning of the final weigh in. Yikes! Nevertheless, I won my money back, and I lost the weight.

The interesting part of this challenge is that, when people initially read it, they were compelled to ask me how they were supposed to lose the weight. I told them that there was no real plan. They had to figure out what would work for them and then do it. Deep down, we all know what we need to do, don't we - strive to become healthy, with a nice physique, friendly appearance, and comfortable manner, by eating right, exercising, losing excess weight and building our confidence.

For those that like challenge, this was an irresistible proposition. Those not so inclined failed to respond or declined.

This, ultimately, is why my challenge-loving participants succeeded. They were up for the challenge!

Will you accept the same challenge and put it in place with your friends and colleagues?

You accept challenge because you are up for it. You are competitive, usually a good sport, and perhaps you are strong because you have learned to be resilient. You win—you win. You lose—you bounce back and try again. Sound familiar?

When you are honest with yourself, develop the right skills, strategize, and work hard, accepting a challenge is easy. You trust your swing!

Just as a healthy body fuels a healthy mind, a mind that's open to challenge is strong and resilient and ready to win in today's competitive workplace.

Sometimes it's not the quest but the challenge it presents that we desire most.

Trust Your Swing

The 7ᵗʰ Hole - **Relationship equity part one: Recognize positive influence**

Surround yourself with people who love life and learn.

If there ever was one overriding principle in golf, it is the principle of course management. There's a lot to consider, such as knowing the problems, or hazards of the course, and knowing how to cope with them in order to score consistently. You have to play smart and position your shots so that you can place the ball in the "A" position—that position which allows the best approach for your next shot.

In the workplace, I have always felt that relationships are the course-management aspect of business. A fulltime position consists of approximately two thousand hours a year spent communicating and working with others. That's a lot of time, so as you can see, it can be extremely important to know the course in terms of relationships. Really knowing the course will help you score well, and that's exactly what I want to have happen in your workplace life.

The goal is to be confident and direct in your work relationships while eliminating the opportunity for confusion. Strive to be effective in all of your relationships, ridding yourself of distracting influences and making the most of the positive ones.

> **Passion in life...is life. It's contagious. Get naked and roll around in it. People who enjoy living have it all figured out. They are passionate, driven, alive, and they are real.**

I have been very fortunate to be surrounded by such passionate people—two of the most amazing people are my parents. They are enthusiastic, warm, generous, and genuine. Growing up, I was encouraged endlessly to do whatever I wanted to do, with one single mandate: Whatever you decide to do, make sure that you are self-supportive. Perfect.

What does this have to do with being successful in the workplace? Everything! One of my colleagues tells a story about how he used to hang out with some of the people from his department. At first, he enjoyed their company, but as they came to know each other better, he found them to be extremely negative and even angry. All they did was complain about their job and gossip about their co-workers. Now, even though my colleague is an upbeat, intelligent person, he would go back to his office down about his work, his company, and even life. He let their negativity affect him without even realizing it. So think about the value of positivity, and then think of how positivity can affect your world.

Surround yourself with people that build you up and make you feel important. Repay them ten times over with the same respect.

If you aspire to be the best at what you do, spend time with the people who will inspire you.

Why? Simple! People that inspire us stimulate and enliven us. They draw out the best in us and fuel our motivation.

Make an effort to spend quality time with people that love life. Passionate people are natural mentors. Pay attention and listen with your heart. These are the people that have it all figured out.

As much as we all have been positively influenced in our lives, there is a tendency to discount the value of these important experiences over time. We're busy, life is chaotic, and our thoughts are focused on the here and now.

From time to time, though, it's important to regroup and try to revisit times when you were exposed to positive influences in your life. Remember any resulting positive life lessons learned and make a point of passing those lessons on when you get the chance.

The following is a brief example of positive life influences.

I was eight. Freshly bathed and dressed in shorts and a T-shirt, I was airlifted to the basement where I was plunked into a huge, brand new, shiny garbage pail containing a secret combination of fresh grapes. I was in heaven!

My dad and uncle had done their research and brought home a trailer load of spectacular grapes from the Niagara region in Ontario. I wanted to eat them all.

I had the honor of squashing the grapes. Although I knew they were humoring me—they thought I would be exhausted or bored in minutes—I eagerly and stubbornly thrashed around in my sweet grape-ness, happy to be a part of the wine-making team.

I grew up with these values.

My parents taught me to work hard, be self-reliant, and above all be myself. They let me join in whenever I showed an interest, and then they would encourage me to jump in with both feet—in some cases literally. I was never too young or just a kid.

Although my dad had a stressful, high-pressure career, he always made time for me. He took time to explain things, what he did at work, different human relations problems he had to deal with, and how critically important his management team was to him. He had a great respect for those that worked smart and worked hard, and I can only imagine that he was effective in letting them know how important they were. I know he always made me feel important. Life was full of opportunities, and life around the dinner table involved listening to stories about life in the working world. He made me feel confident that I could do anything I wanted to do in business and in life.

My mom was the family architect and landscape specialist. She designed several houses and cottages over the years. All innocent bystanders were quickly recruited, handed a hammer, and it was game on. The old "get your hands dirty and get things done" adage was the motto of the day. Everyone who helped them knew that payback was a given. You help us and we'll help you. It was reciprocity at its best! In fact, my dad was always the first guy ready to help anyone. He was the go-to guy! There wasn't much that he wouldn't tackle, and he was known to have the best-stocked shop in town. If he didn't have the part or piece of the puzzle on hand to do a repair, he would make it. He would get things done!

I always had freedom. I had freedom to explore, freedom to make mistakes, and freedom to learn from my mistakes. I guess this is part of the "three off the tee" mentality, and of course, why I like it. You screw up sometimes, but you learn from it and move forward.

If you're not afraid of working hard, self-reliance comes easy!

My parents were near forty with two teenage boys when I was born. I used to joke that I grew up with three dads, but I actually learned a lot from growing up in a family of adults. I never wanted to be the little sister that was never quite old enough, smart enough, or strong enough. I always saw myself as an equal, and I busted my ass to keep up. What an incredible sense of motivation I knew at such a young age.

My brothers and I, under our dad's supervision, bought car wrecks to rebuild. We learned that if you invested blood and sweat fixing something, you sure as hell took care of it. This is where my good work ethic was born.

One thing in particular that stands out in my mind is the many summers spent at our cottage in Georgian Bay. Every weekend meant getting together with friends and family. We had fish fries, pig roasts, sailing regattas, and cardboard boat races. There were volleyball tournaments during the day and guitar playing and singing by the fire at night on the beach. Being exposed to friends, family, and neighbors of all ages, getting together and truly enjoying one another's company, was a great awakening for me. It taught me how to interact well with others. Deep down we are all the same. We want to be heard and we want to feel important. This is one of the most valuable things to remember in the workplace. Encourage others to be involved, as what they have to say is important.

There is a gift given freely by some people. They are special. They are mentors. They touch your mind, and you carry them with you for the rest of your life. The lessons they pass on are invaluable and can play an integral part in the person you become. For me, there have been so many positive people in my life...

   o The older brothers that motivated me to keep up

o The teachers and professors who repeatedly went out of their way to encourage and challenge me

o The bosses that gave me the opportunity to prove what I could do

o The many colleagues I know that have my back

o The husband that encourages me to chase my dreams (I cannot begin to explain how important this is.)

o The daughter that impresses me more every single day

One of my favorite stories, as told to me by my grandmother, dates back to 1928 when she was a young mother of four children, ranging in age from one to six. They lived on a hundred-acre parcel of land in a small farming community of Ontario.

Back then, life was hard. Her days were consumed with cleaning, raising children, making clothes, baking, and farming. It's astounding to think back to just how hard life was back then and how, today, we take everyday modern conveniences for granted.

On this one particular day, my grandmother was already physically exhausted, but she left the house, stepped into a heavy wooden neck brace that carried two large buckets, and headed off down the long, rocky, wooded trail that led to their well.

She quickly filled the buckets and set them on top of a large rock so she could hook them with the brace to carry them back to the house. Then, as she struggled to lift them off the rock, she spotted a baby black bear just off to her left.

Immediately, she thought that the mother had to be nearby, and she was. The mother bear was off to her right, and she knew it wasn't good to be caught between a mother bear and her cub.

Exhausted and weighted down with the heavy wooden neck brace that now held the two full buckets of water, she looked back and forth at the bears.

As only my grandmother could put it—she looked directly at the mother bear and said, "Well, you're just gonna have to eat me!"

She struggled under the weight of the load, shifting the brace on her shoulders, then slowly walked home and never saw the bears again.

My grandmother was one direct, spunky, hard-working woman. This story is just a mere example of her bravery and grit, but I can tell you first hand that she was a powerhouse. As exhausted and worn out as she was, she had to keep going. Others were waiting for her, counting on her, and things had to get done.

Whenever I feel that I'm caught between a rock and a hard place (pun intended), I remember this story, smile to myself, and know that I can face whatever hazard is in my way.

Whenever anyone is willing to give his or her time to you, make the time to listen. It's the old saying: "If I only knew then what I know now"…well, I'd do things differently—smarter and better. You just never know when someone is going to pass on a piece of knowledge to you that will create a positive impact in your world. By reliving instances of positive influences in your life, you cultivate a positive mind and a successful life.

People who love life know the value of positive influence. They are the pros!

Trust Your Swing

The 8th Hole - **Relationship equity part two: Communicate fairly**

Send and receive.

When you effectively manage your golf game, you make course management and mental game techniques work to your advantage. You are playing smart, you trust your swing, and you are upgrading your performance level. The same is true in the workplace. Your work game relates to knowing the nature of the relationship and the role required of you. If you want to move forward and develop better relationships, you need to know what you want and how to cultivate the relationship through better communication skills.

There's a ton of books about how to communicate better—with your spouse, with your boss, with your co-workers. I'm not going to go into a long-winded explanation about how to communicate; I just want you to be very aware that to be successful in business, you need to communicate fairly. It's a simple process. Think before you talk. It's planning your shot—know what you are dealing with and make your best play.

The "communicate fairly" rules.

I put communication under the idea of relationships because communication takes two people. One person starts the conversation and another person receives it. However, there are a million things that can go wrong in that simple formula, in both personal and business communication. For example, the person sending the communication doesn't really like the person on the other end. The person receiving the communication is not paying attention and doesn't really want to get the communication he or she is being given. The list goes on and on.

In any communication situation, you are both the sender and the receiver, and when you're communicating fairly, you expect certain things to happen as you play both roles. To help you communicate fairly, I've put together a list of my favorite communication rules to help you play— or communicate—fairly. Here they are:

1) *Pay attention to what people are saying to you.* It's not enough just to listen when people are talking. You need to pay particular attention to the nonverbal elements in speech, such as body language, hand gestures, vocal tone, and emotional state. Actively read their demeanor and listen to their responses. Try to ascertain if they, in fact, are being straightforward and truthful in their conversation as opposed to just saying what they think you want to hear.

2) *Speak for comfort.* If you use words that are too big for the topic, spew out too much information, talk too fast, or fail to articulate effectively, you will lose the attention of the listener. The best form of communication is crisp and clear.

3) *When you talk to people, really take the time to listen and get what they're trying to say to you.* Most communication books will tell you that listening is something of a lost art. Nevertheless, fair communication means you listen to what's being said to you. People love being heard.

    a. How do you listen effectively? First, you acknowledge when someone is speaking to you. Have you ever known someone who just talks and talks? I have, and I found that if I acknowledge them by saying simple things like, "I got it," or "I understand," or even, "I heard you," it lets them know that I really did hear what they were saying. This doesn't mean that you agree with them; it just means that you have heard what they said.

b. Another great listening technique is to ask questions. I talk about that in the next rule, but just know that the process of asking questions demonstrates that you are listening and interested in the person you are speaking with, which reinforces that relationship. The more you focus on listening, the better you will get at it.

4) *Ask questions.* Asking skillful questions is an amazing and effective communication tool. By asking for information, you effectively eliminate the opportunity of assumption or speculation on your part, while you learn the truth about what others are thinking and feeling.

a. Ask at least one direct and relevant question before voicing your opinion. This opens up discussion and removes the risk of people feeling that you are trying to force your attitude or opinion on them. Take note of how people respond, both verbally and through body language, to what you have to say.

b. Ask questions that effectively deal with any preconceived assumptions you may have. Keep asking questions until the answers received leave you considering the facts only.

c. Be polite and open. Encourage discussion and promote understanding and interest. Be careful not to appear to be too forceful. Be aware of your voice, body language, and choice of words.

5) *Decide if it's worth the fight.* Take the temperature of the person you are about to talk to. Is the person in a good mood and comfortable? It may be better to postpone serious discussion if the timing is bad.

a. Use your abilities to shift feelings positively. Ask thoughtful questions, show respect for others, boost morale, encourage involvement, and reduce stress.

b. Sometimes people have intense feelings that may predate their current relationship. If they have sensitive or anxiety-driven feelings, you can develop nurturing regimes and interests that do not demand so much from them. By allowing others to answer questions, you allow them to stay in charge of themselves even when you are guiding them. They can face the mirror instead of defending themselves. This is necessary and especially potent with people who harbor memories of abuse. They develop self-preserving mechanisms to protect themselves and may find it difficult to open up and communicate comfortably.

c. Sometimes people have strong attitudes that need to be reworked. If you come across as being too aggressive, demanding, or offensive, you can force others to shut down. For example, if you use expressions that demand change, your words may pack an additional punch that could be perceived as an attack. For example, when someone says, "If you had done your work earlier...I would have made my deadline," they imply that it's your fault that they didn't make their deadline.

At this point, the hair stands up on your neck because you are angered by the perceived accusation and you feel that you are being manipulated into believing that you are in some way at fault.

By reworking attitudes, we can be more direct and effective in our style. Perhaps a new approach such as, "It would really help if you could get your portion of the project done by this date so that we can all make our deadline," would be a little more effective and a lot less antagonistic.

6) *Sometimes you have to let others win.* We human beings are funny creatures. We like to be right, so much so that we'll sometimes go to great lengths to be right about things. However, being right to the point of making someone else wrong doesn't foster good communication. Sometimes the power you relinquish by letting someone else be right can open up the conversation so that you can learn more about what others think and feel. Try to set the tone by being blatantly honest and letting down your guard. This is not a sign of weakness, but rather a sign of trust and openness.

---

a. Think about what changes you can make in your approach to take pressure off a topic of contention. Try looking at the issues that cause aggravation for those people with whom you have to work. Sometimes a simple change in time schedules that reduces the urgency to get things done can reduce pressure in such a way as to reduce the stress in the relationship. Whenever you take the initiative to calm things down, you let others chill out and regroup. You can endeavor to let them have the upper hand and regain perspective.

b. Keep in mind also that no one is perfect. Sometimes willingness to accept another person's shortcomings is a more powerful move toward resolution than talking about those shortcomings will ever be. Actions speak louder than words.

7) *If something is important to you, discuss it face to face.* This is the #1 problem in business. People like to hide behind e-mail and texting, and the phone is always a convenient way not to talk face to face with someone. Don't hide. If a situation or relationship is important to you, meet the

person involved and discuss things until there is resolution. You may discover a completely new perspective on the situation at hand when you physically see how others react to what is being discussed.

8) *If you find that you are endlessly caught in the same argument, act.* This means act first, and communicate later. Find the solution, fix the problem first, and then discuss why it happened after the fact, with the sole intent of ensuring that it never happens again.

9) *Know that asking is more effective than telling.* Nobody likes being lectured. You can be much more effective in finding solutions if you ask probing questions and allow others to find their own solutions by thinking things through.

10) *Get to the root of the problem.* Big issues sometimes evolve from oversights that stem from your inability or even refusal to be aware. Problems don't fix themselves, and they can escalate if unaddressed. Work toward gaining understanding of the situation—communicate, and resolve.

11) *Be aware and beware.* Be aware of unsolicited denials. If someone is going out of

his way to deny something, he just may be guilty. This is your heads up to beware.

12) *Challenge yourself to ask more questions when interacting with others.* You will improve your overall communication skills, strengthen your relationships, and reduce misinterpretations. Record the facts on a notepad. What pieces of real information have you gained through your conversations? This encourages you to eliminate assumptions, which in turn reinforces a fusion of understanding and accountability. You need to ask for information, confirm, and clarify that you have interpreted it correctly, and then, if any action is required, ensure that everyone is clear about what needs to be done and by whom.

Ultimately, good communicators make time to effectively and openly acknowledge the good in others. They praise, compliment, and encourage others to feel good about themselves.

In the event of a communication breakdown, decide whether you will dwell in the negative or rise above the angst and turmoil in a firm, positive manner and encourage all parties to listen and be heard.

Trust Your Swing

The 9th Hole - Utilize your strengths

It's all about using your strengths in order to be consistent!

Try as you might, you are never going to excel at everything. We all have strengths and weaknesses. Those who appear to be the strongest, however, are the people who know how to best use their strengths to camouflage their perceived weaknesses. They do this by emphasizing their strengths as well as utilizing their strengths to compensate for their weaknesses. They know the value of being consistent and reliable. It's all about creating and projecting the persona that is consistent overall, even though some abilities or traits may still require some tweaking, strengthening, and improvement.

This leads to the importance of going to the driving range—the self-improvement plan—and then the actual game, where you utilize your strengths to make your best play!

At the driving range, your practice and hard work are what develop your consistency!

In golf, if you want to break 100, 90, 80, or 70, you need to be consistent. This means that you can repeatedly make the same shot on demand. Obviously, the better you are at being consistent, the lower your score will be. The five most important fundamentals that lead to consistency are your grip, your ball position, your alignment, your tension level, and your balance from address to the end of your follow-through. The best place to strengthen your abilities and develop your proficiency is at the driving range. Many people have their favorite practice and warm-up drills and swear by them. I generally use my "Hit 'til you're happy" drill as follows:

1) Warm up by stretching and swinging loosely for at least five minutes.

2) Take a large bucket of balls and start hitting my clubs from shortest to longest.

3) Take a practice swing with the club, and then hit balls until I'm happy. Usually, this means five solid, clean shots, well executed

with proper direction. Then I move on to the next club and repeat the process until I reach my driver. (I always save my driver for last, as it is my favorite club, and I usually try to be as efficient as I can during the drill so that I have a lot of balls left to enjoy! Woo hoo!)

4) Finally, when I run out of balls, I head to the practice green to work on chipping and putting, until I'm happy.

I tell you this because, in this way, I can calculate my consistency. For example, if I have to hit ten balls in order to hit five that I am happy with, then my consistency is only 50 percent. My overall consistency is a more meaningful percentage, but I can still use my club-by-club analysis to see where I need to improve. Therefore, the next time out, I can focus on hitting the clubs that I am not as consistent with more often, in order to upgrade my overall consistency percentage.

We all have strengths that we try to accentuate whenever possible. It's the put-your-best-foot-forward mentality. Sometimes, we also use our strengths to camouflage a self-perceived weakness. Really, that's okay, too. At that place in time, you are again trying to put your best foot forward.

Now this is what happens when you hit the golf course. You are no longer in practice mode. At this point, it's game on. So, for example, if you are slicing the ball repeatedly, you need to try to make some adjustments as you play and compensate as best you can. A number of circumstances could be affecting your game. You may not have had time to warm up, or perhaps you are feeling rushed. The point is, on the golf course, your focus is on course management and scoring well. You need to use your strengths to make this happen. Take your best shot! Later, at the driving range, you can use your notes from your game scorecard detailing your mishits and work on fixing them.

Therefore, as you can see, it's very important to know what you are doing right, where you excel, and how to use your strengths to your advantage. In addition, it's equally important to recognize your weaknesses, those low-consistency areas where you can work toward building yourself up to gain a higher consistency rating overall.

The same stands true in the workplace. You need to develop an overall consistency of professionalism and the right skill sets. You need to assess your strengths and weaknesses honestly. Then you can use your strengths to compensate for your weaknesses or shortcomings until you are able to strengthen them. Perhaps further education, training, or experience is required to take you to the next level.

If you are just starting out in the workplace, you come with aspirations of greatness and dreams of glory. You have a general plan and are anxious to jump in with both feet and start learning. You are anxious to transform from the "new guy or girl" into a business-savvy contender, ready to take on whatever comes your way.

Well, come out swinging, as they say, and show everyone what you've got! It's the old "it won't go in if it can't get there" analogy. If you don't show us your strengths, we can't see you. To get where you are at this point, you have impressed some- one. That person has given you an opportunity. Perhaps your resume, your confidence, or your business sense opened the door for you, but now it's up to you to keep that door open.

It's not enough to be educated, or even knowl- edgeable, for that matter. You need to know the importance of developing relationships, whether they are with customers, colleagues, or superiors. You consistently need to show that you can use your strengths effectively. Focus on presenting yourself as being involved, prepared, capable, and willing. Practice at being the one that every- one knows will get the job done right.

If you dread ending up in the bunker, practice these tricky out-of-the-sand shots until you master them. Think of it as insurance—we all

---

have learned that, once you know you can make that shot easily, you will seldom need to!

So, let's look at the workplace and what doing it right is all about. If you want to advance, you need to know that there are definite, notable traits that are associated with being promotable. See how you stack up against the following list, and think about how you can learn how to incorporate these traits into the workplace "you."

These are the main traits to shoot for:

Be energetic:

This is the ability to focus on the project at hand and get results. A person that is energetic and usually confident and charismatic is willing to accept challenge with optimism and ease.

Be likeable and approachable:

The ability to cultivate strong relationships is crucial, not only within the workplace, but also when dealing with customers or clients. Remember that the concept that "we are all in customer service" never gets old. Customer service is, moreover, why we have a job in the first place. Being able to interact fairly and effectively with a variety of people is the essence of being a good communicator as well as a good leader.

Use your intellect:

This is the ability to learn and then use what you've learned to make knowledgeable, unbiased decisions, which makes you effective and results oriented. The more that you are open to learn, the more you flex your abilities and the better your results. It's a process.

Invest your time:

This is the willingness to offer and dedicate your time and effort to meet corporate goals.

Promote synergy:

This is the ability and desire to cultivate teamwork, knowing that the efforts of the team could well surpass the efforts of the individual.

Dress the part:

This means know the dress code for your particular workplace and dress accordingly. Always aim for the high side, though—dressed well but not overdressed. Dressing well reinforces that you are promotable in two distinct ways. It shows that your work is important to you and that you will be able to transform or climb the corporate ladder with ease, since you already visualize yourself as an achiever on the upward track.

We are drawn to people that are similar to us, as they make us feel comfortable and accepted. We are attracted to people that compliment us, as they make us feel good about ourselves. We are challenged by people that inspire us, as they open our eyes to opportunity. And we are encouraged by people that have achieved their goals, since they let us see that we can do the same. These people rise to the top.

Congratulations!

You've just finished your front nine! In the front nine, we've dealt with all of the basics of improving the "self." These include how you see yourself, your attitude, your ability to learn, your willingness to push through barriers, your motivation to make good decisions, your confidence level, your desire to accept challenge, your awareness of positive influence, your communication skills, and how you use your strengths.

When you trust your swing, you trust yourself. You have the basics, the right attitude and motivation to make things happen. Now you're ready for the back nine, where the focus is on putting all the basics into play in the workplace and your personalized pursuit of success.

The right attitude is everything!

At the Turn
Know What You Want

In golf, when you finish your front nine, you are traditionally "at the turn." It's the time to take a breather, grab a refreshment—whatever you can sneak in—and then it's time to rush back and get started on the back nine.

For a while now, I've been talking about attitudes and improving yourself in order to succeed. Now, for your breather, I want you to reflect on what you want out of your work life. I will give you a quick recap of helpful information to get you ready for the back nine.

People today, more than ever, are stepping up and taking charge of their lives. There is a new cultural openness toward how we live our lives, and we are living our lives to the fullest. We know that we are entitled to our own time as individuals and that we are free to pursue our dreams and desires in an effort to figure out what is important to us.

Sometimes, though, we are so caught up in what we don't want in our lives that we are sidetracked and lose our focus—we are stuck.

The important thing to do is to take a minute to write down what you *do* want. How can you improve your score if you don't accurately keep your score? It's the same thing. How can you get what you want if you don't know what you want? Figure it out!

Now, here's the secret. Once you finally figure it all out and know what you want—expect nothing less!

It's all about knowing what you want in the workplace or what workplace success means to you.

Here's a list to get you in the right frame of thought:

o Workplace/Workspace Camaraderie— Face it, most of us spend more time with co-workers than we do with friends and family. Getting along with co-workers can make the difference between enjoying your time spent at work and just putting in time.

o Job Satisfaction—Feeling challenged, fulfilled, important, appreciated, and promotable are all part of the stimuli that bring about job satisfaction. What factors are the most important to you?

o Corporate Community—Find the right corporate environment to suit you. Aside from working within the field of your expertise, the company attitude also plays an important factor in how you will fit in. For example, if you have high expectations of climbing the corporate ladder, you better make sure that there is a good fit between you and the company and that there is in fact going to be a position that could potentially open up for you within a time frame suitable for you. For example, if the only position you could migrate into is presently held by one of the owners—chances are you're not going to have the opportunity to be promoted into that position, unless you are hoping to become a partner or if the owner is planning to retire.

o   Respect—Mutual respect in the workplace is crucial. Getting along with your bosses, colleagues, and/or co-workers because you genuinely like and respect them is nothing short of amazing. There is no room for complacency. Creativity and team focus run rampant.

Now focus on what you want:

1)   You have a choice of what career path you take, and you can change midstream if you find something more suitable to what you want to do.

2) You don't "need" to follow anyone's example, and you don't have to follow a stereotypical career path. Realize your entrepreneurial flair.

3) You don't "need" to stick with the same career all of your life. Sometimes opportunities come your way. Sometimes you will find that your skills also work well in different areas where you could progress more quickly or where you feel more challenged.

4) Take time to figure out what you want and need. Do this on a regular basis and address what *is* and *isn't* working for you, and then make changes accordingly.

The Back Nine
The Pursuit
of Success

Risk vs. Reward

The 10th Hole: Develop your business role

The 11th Hole: Strategize to get ahead

The 12th Hole: Deal with expectations

The 13th Hole: Empower yourself and others

The 14th Hole: Be proactive

The 15th Hole: Learn from the change-ready
company

The 16th Hole: Cultivate team spirit

The 17th Hole: Take the initiative to lead

The 18th Hole: Succeed in the workplace

In "The Front Nine," we dealt with various attitudes you need to adopt in order to be successful. In this section, I want to look at some of the success strategies you can adopt to help you move up the success ladder faster—some strategies for competitive play.

As you pursue your work goals, I want you to be acutely aware of one very important fact: In whatever you do, it's crucial to analyze the amount of risk you might take and then establish whether the potential reward for your actions is worth it.

In golf, when you trust your swing, use solid course management skills, and know you can make the shot with confidence, you know that the risk is worth the reward. In a high-risk situation, golf professionals are generally only willing to take risks when necessary to win. High-risk play is dangerous, so usually the best play is to play smart. The pros strategize; they take calculated risks in order to stay in the hunt (the game), play smart, and win.

One powerful lesson to be learned from golf is to deal with one hazard at a time. As I said before, the game is broken down into eighteen holes, each with its own challenges, so each shot is dealt with independently. A golfer that shoots par effectively takes a round of golf and turns it into seventy-two independent segments (assuming that you are playing a standard par 72 course). He focuses on playing his best shot, dealing with the hazard at hand, and deciding where he wants his ball to lie (where the ball finishes) in order to set up for the next shot.

The same stands true when we look at how to succeed in business. You look at each challenge individually. You approach it with a healthy and positive self-perception, strong, developed interpersonal skills, and the business acumen required to get the job done right.

You step up and take the challenge, knowing what the risk is and whether that risk is worth the reward of success on a play-by-play basis. If it is worth the risk, you go for it!

"The Back Nine" deals with putting all that you know into play. In golf, part of your strategizing involves knowing how to work the ball using the arsenal of fourteen weapons you carry in your golf bag—your putter, irons, and woods. Think of the clubs as business skills. "The Back Nine" deals with making sure that you are well armed with the right tools to make the shot. Whether on the golf course or in the workplace, you need to know how to win!

Swing Thoughts:

Decide where you want to fit
in within the corporation.

Develop winning skill sets.

Climb the leader board (a
scoreboard showing the top
performers in a competition,
particularly a golf tournament).

Risk vs. Reward

The 10ᵗʰ Hole - **Develop your business role**

Employee, employer, or entrepreneur— what will I be?

It is often said that the game of golf is 90 percent mental. This means that to score well, or be successful on the golf course, 90 percent of what it takes comes from how you "think" your way around the course. It's all about developing a single and predominant focus while effectively multitasking. So here, you're in your pre-shot routine. You go through the process of reading the hole, knowing where your best target is, knowing how you are playing that particular day, and how confident you are of your abilities. You make an educated decision on how to play the shot. This is the single and predominant focus. The mental aspect of the pre-shot routine revolves around staying focused on the intended target while, at the same time, multitasking—assessing hazards, the lie, yardage to your target, the right club to use, and wind force and direction.

Ultimately, you will choose a play that makes you comfortable, a play that you know is achievable and right for you, considering your current abilities. This is not about just going through the motions. This is about getting your head into the game and knowing your best play given your current abilities for every shot you take. The same is true of defining the right business role for yourself. It's important to know your interests, your expertise, your talents, your strengths, and your current abilities. You need to know what you are capable of now and how you plan to progress in the future—your career path. That being said, if you're just starting out in the workplace, it's sometimes hard to have a clear focus or even be fully aware of your abilities until you get out in the workplace and get your feet wet.

Why is it that we must choose a career path when we are so green, lacking work-life experience?

I laugh to myself when I think back to my early career choices. First, I wanted to grow up to be an archaeologist, then a rock star, and later a psychologist.

At a young age, my brothers and I were set loose in the wilds on Northern Ontario. Being somewhat of a tomboy, it was nothing for me to drag home an animal carcass or loose bones. I once discovered an animal skull in the woods by our weekend farmhouse. I took it home and scrubbed it with my new toothbrush and some bleach to whiten and clean it. We later identified it as a baby bear skull. It was undoubtedly the most interesting show-and-tell item at school that year and, at that point, I was certain that I wanted to be an archaeologist.

Later, somewhere in and around eight years old, I developed a keen interest in music. A door-to-door sales representative stopped at our house one night. I was found to have an incredible ear for music and exceptionally long fingers best suited to playing none other than the accordion! Yes, and I played right into the whole sales strategy, knowing in my heart that someday I would go on to be a musical prodigy.

After a month of serious good behavior and chronic begging, my mom and dad caved and signed me up for music lessons. A few months later, they bought me the accordion of my dreams, shiny, black, and beautiful. I'm certain it weighed more than I did and I could barely see over the top of it, but I would never dare complain. Back in the day, this was a huge purchase for my parents, and I continued to take lessons until the eighth grade when I switched to playing piano and then guitar. It was at that point that I realized that I was destined to be a rock star. I just knew it!

By the time I hit my mid-teens, I noticed that people seemed compelled to tell me their private feelings and secrets. I remember wondering why they were telling me this stuff. Maybe it was because I was generally interested in people and what makes them tick. I asked many questions that indirectly forced people to answer their own questions. I have honed this skill over the years. It's very effective, yet, at the same time, very annoying for those who are on to me. At this point in my life, though, I began to consider the prospect of becoming a psychologist. To me it seemed to be an obvious fit.

Do you have a career path in mind or are you figuring it out as you go?

The point to my little digression on "what I wanted to be when I grew up" really comes from an important question that you have to ask yourself as you move forward in business. Some of you may be doing exactly what you thought you would be when you were eight or nine. Others of you are probably at the polar opposite end, and many of you are somewhere in between. However, no matter what you are doing, there is one other "role" issue that no one asks about, let alone addresses.

The question, simply, is how do you see yourself fitting into the business world? Are you an employee, employer, or do you bring entrepreneurial skills to your workplace?

A lot of the time, when you are first starting out in the workplace, it comes down to trial and error. You try to be selective about which types of companies you apply to and ask many questions so that you know what you are getting into. You won't really know if you have made a good choice, however, until you have the job and have been working there for a while. The influx of new experiences and opportunities, coupled with the challenge of learning to interact with a variety of personalities, from co-workers to colleagues to superiors and even customers, all work together to create the environment of the company. The most important thing for an employee is to gel with a company. He or she needs to fit in, feel challenged, and be able to recognize the corporate migration path available to the most qualified person.

There is no one right way. Just figure out what works for you!

In golf, you choose the play that makes you comfortable, considering your current abilities. It's the same in the workplace. You choose the role that you are most comfortable in at the time. There is no one right way, and it is important to note that the role you are most comfortable in today may change dramatically over the years as you progress along your career path.

As an employee, you may enjoy your work and feel challenged and motivated. You may like the stability of knowing that you have a steady paycheck, benefits, and regular scheduled vacation time. If you can see that there is a defined path for you to advance within the company and it fits with your career requirements, then you may be happy for a long time. Larger corporations offer structure and a multitude of excellent opportunities that will fit well within your career comfort zone.

On the other hand, if you are comfortable choosing a career path that may be somewhat less secure and perhaps more risk oriented, where you make the decisions and take charge, flexing your entrepreneurial spirit may appeal to you. You may choose to either start a new business or buy an established one to build upon.

Again, the right business role for you is the one that you choose. There is no one right or wrong way!

Read corporate culture.

Typically, businesses are best described as being hierarchical organizations. Decisions are made at the top. The corporate culture, direction, and motivation are devised and revised at a high level.

The problem with such an organizational structure is that it does not promote collaboration. People in middle management tend to resist top management if they are placed in the position of enforcing a corporate strategy that they have not been a part of developing. They feel that they are policing the process rather than being an active participant.

There also becomes a tendency for some to back off and feel disassociated when they know that senior management have made decisions without their consideration. This is especially true when they have firsthand knowledge of the day-to-day operations or processes involved.

That being said, hierarchical organizations do need entrepreneurial-minded employees that like new challenges and experiences and that are comfortable with taking risks. They also need dedicated and involved management staff who want to play an active role within the company.

To address this type of hierarchical deficiency, some organizations develop a decentralized business model that encourages autonomy and initiative. Employees need to become an integral and intrinsic part of the corporate culture, and these businesses recognize that there needs to be incentive for employees to become involved, be accountable, and feel challenged.

Businesses need to develop an environment where employees can fit in easily, feel challenged, and effectively take on a role that fits in with the overall company objectives. They need to be aware of those that are willing to go the extra distance: the employees that possess an entrepreneurial spirit at work and the ones that dig in and get results. If there is a corporate culture present to support such ideals, the employee with entrepreneurial flair will continue to feel challenged and involved.

When, however, businesses fail to provide this type of corporate culture, they face the challenge of being able to attract and retain talented people. Employees that are deemed to have an entrepreneurial flair usually thrive on having the freedom to use their creativity, charisma, and enthusiasm at their discretion. They are focused, intuitive, and driven, and when you couple their attention to detail with solid business sense, they manifest a truly dynamic force. Although being an entrepreneur is not synonymous with being successful, it is often the case. It is in the best interest of the business to be able to attract and keep such talented and insightful people.

As every company develops its own corporate culture and sense of community, it is important for you to find the best fit for you. Your best plan of attack is to test the waters. Figure out what you want, decide which business role best suits your requirements, and then set your course.

Consider the value of doing what you love and being paid for it! This is truly a golfer's dream.

Risk vs. Reward

The 11th Hole - **Strategize to get ahead**

Follow a structured, strategic plan to achieve agreed-on goals.

If you don't know what you're up against, you can't plan. If you can't plan, you can't win. This is true on the golf course, and it's true for every other aspect of life. In golf, your ultimate goal is to lower your score—quite simply, a low score means success. To get there, you need a practice plan or strategy in order to define how you are going to achieve your goal. You need to know what clubs to hit, how far you hit the ball with them, and how proficient you are at working the ball to your advantage. You can use a drill like my "Hit until you're happy drill" from the 9th hole, for example. Perhaps your swing thought should be "Success, oh yeah!" You can focus two-thirds of your time on your short game (one hundred-yard radius from the pin) and the other third on long game practice. This is relevant, as two-thirds of a round of golf is generally focused on your short game. You can also use your score or green cards to analyze previous rounds played, in order to target what you need to practice. There is so much that you can do, that is, if you have a plan!

I'm sure you're all familiar with the importance of setting goals. However, not everyone writes them down, and I've often wondered why that is. Is it because you're afraid you're not going to reach them? Whatever the reason, it doesn't really matter. What does matter is that you need to find a way to make goals work for you, and while I'm not going into a whole long diatribe about how to effectively set goals, perhaps what I'm about to tell you will enable you to wrap your head around the process.

Dream but don't be a dreamer.

It's funny. Our Western work culture tends to frown on the idea of dreaming, as though it is a waste of time. I think that's all wrong. Having a dream is the precursor to making something happen—be it little or great. Dreams and ideas inspire and push us to challenge the status quo. Now, being a *dreamer,* on the other hand, someone that talks about his or her dreams but never does anything about them, well, there's the waste of time. This is where those without a real plan have let their dreams slip right through their fingers, leaving them with nothing better to talk about than what they "could have" done.

So, how do you dream without falling into "dreamer" status? Start by defining your career. Then add in your lifestyle and your home-style, and start living the dream. Even though this is a book about work success, it is always important to remember that work life and home life are not completely separate. If you're happy at work, chances are you're going to be happier at home—and vice versa.

To dream realistically, here's something you need to keep in mind: Be flexible and regroup as required. but stick to the overall plan. In other words, you need a plan, first, and you need to have a firm overall goal in mind, but then the rest is all about seeing what works, what doesn't, and fixing the plan as you go.

One of the most effective ways I have found to do all of that is through benchmarking. To make your dreams a reality, you analyze the process required to get you there and then break it down into manageable and controllable segments. You can be as detailed as you want while remaining flexible if you start out with a high-level approach and then tighten up as you start to see your progress and direction evolve.

To help you benchmark your career, I'm giving you the typical benchmarks I have seen repeatedly as people move through their life cycles:

Sixteen to Twenty-Five Years: The Education Cycle

This is the time to try everything. It's the only real way to discover what you want to do. Education extends beyond schooling to include travel, learning new languages and cultures, and trying new things outside of your comfort zone.

The hardest thing to do is to decide what you want to do for the rest of your life. One of the best options, though, is to keep your options open. For example, if you really don't have an absolute career in mind, focus on getting a solid business education so that you have the basics. In whatever you do in your life, a good business sense will always be an asset.

Twenty-Six to Thirty-Five Years: The Making-it Cycle

This is the time to work hard, pay your dues, and kick your life into gear. If you're not really rocking by the time you're thirty, you're in for some tough sledding. The movers and shakers are making it all happen by thirty-five, and they are ready to shine.

Thirty-Six to Forty-Five: The Performance Cycle

You are now at your peak and claiming the world as your own. You've got it all figured out and you are playing out your dream.

Forty-Six-Plus Years: Success

For some, you've reached your success. You are now mentor material. Make time to coach.

As I mentioned, these are benchmarks—a guide. This is not to say that, somewhere along the line, you won't just lose your mind and go through a full-blown "career crisis" where you find your-self looking for something new, something more challenging. People today more than ever are really seeking out what they want in life. We are healthier than ever, living longer, and feel very capable of starting a new career or even a new career-lifestyle, such as running vacation charters in the Caribbean after spending a career lifetime crunching numbers for a living.

Also today, many people are being displaced. They have lost what they once thought were secure and permanent positions and have found themselves starting out again looking for a new job. Such career rebirths can also lead us in totally new and exciting directions.

Strategies to help you plan more effectively at work

Now that you have some of the big-picture stuff, it's time to look at some of the particulars to help you be successful reaching those benchmarks:

o Decipher and digest the game plan of your company. What is the overall objective, the result required, and, most importantly, what is your role in the execution of the plan? What approaches and/or tools can be used to achieve specific goals? Do you really want it?

o Practice what you preach—once you have clearly identified what you need to do to improve your potential for success, put it into play. Do a presentation in front of a mirror— check your expression and posture—are you comfortable? Your ease or lack of ease will affect how your audience feels about what you have to say.

o What is your working aptitude? You will undoubtedly excel in an area or field where you can use your strengths. Seek new responsibilities or roles where your traits suit what is needed.

o Adapt your communication style to fit your work environment and your career path. Your vocabulary, tone of voice, presence, and overall manner of communicating ideas and requests are crucial to how you are perceived and how others will respond to you.

o Know the facts and stick to the facts. This speaks to your competence and your credibility. Take time to do research, figure things out, and relay those facts to others. You only have to be caught in a mistruth or exaggeration once to tarnish your integrity and the way you are perceived.

o Recognize that your personal life needs to coincide with and compliment your work ethic and political persona. People build opinions about who you are based on you as a whole person. They consider all that they know about you and mesh this with what they expect from you.

In golf, as in life, it's really all about positioning and balance. On each shot, you have to have proper set-up, alignment, and ball position. Each key aspect is as important as the other, and they are all necessary. The proof shows on your score-card. Without a record or benchmark, we may not recognize our deficiencies. Without constructive feedback, we may not continue to improve through learning. Without strength, control, and direction, we may become totally lost and complacent.

Benchmarking allows us to stay focused over the long haul when we use a broad course of direction. It lets us celebrate interim successes and allows us the flexibility and freedom to embrace our entrepreneurial flair. Sometimes following a fork in the road forces us to learn more than we bargained for. The trick is in always knowing how to find your way back.

Risk vs. Reward

The 12th Hole - **Deal with expectations**

Develop appropriate expectations and a quality code of ethics.

At age twenty-seven, I was hired as the controller for a manufacturing company with plants of operation in Canada and the United States. The first year was hectic as I learned the ropes and was looking to make my mark.

The following spring, we had a company-wide meeting of the minds. It was a senior-management-training week held at a nearby resort a couple of weeks prior to our busy season.

I was well aware that there would be a series of meetings to kick off the year, but no one had mentioned that I was expected to deliver a speech on the morning of the first day. I only found this out when I was reading the agenda in my hotel room the night before.

Hmmm…

As it turns out, one of my colleagues and a known nemesis had neglected to mention this to me. In golf, he would be referred to as a sandbagger—a golfer who lies about his golf abilities in order to have the upper hand and, therefore, be able to win because of it. (Sandbagger is a euphemism for a liar or cheater and demonstrates a general lack of integrity.) My co-worker was seriously trying to make me look like a fool on a very important day for me. I can only imagine that in some warped way, in his mind, he felt that he had set me up for failure, which would make him appear better or more professional.

I quickly asked around to find out what I should be talking about in my speech. I found that several of the managers had prepared short videos and presentations. I had no time.

I locked myself away in my hotel room that night and started to write. I knew that, in the past, when I had written about something important to me, it usually was important to others as well. At that time, I had some things I wanted to talk about with our group.

The next morning, the same colleague inquired smugly about the topic of my speech. I told him that I was going to talk about expectations. He strongly suggested that I should rethink this as I was surely going to make a fool of myself, but I didn't listen. I really didn't respect him, and so I wasn't concerned about what he had to say.

Somehow, at that point, I knew exactly what I needed to do. I knew that I brought a wealth of knowledge and expertise to the table. I knew how to find solutions, get my team on board, and get results. I knew that I was working for a company owned and operated by a formidable entrepreneur. I trusted that I was a good judge of character and that our fearless leader would understand what I wanted to address. I knew that he expected nothing less than fearless leadership from his team and that I would not disappoint him.

I was nervous, very nervous, but I struggled through my speech taking time to make eye contact, smile, and make every one of my carefully planned points:

1) I explained that when I had decided to join the company, it was for a very specific reason. It wasn't about money or vacation time or progressing my career path, it was about finding a company that met my expectations.

2) I was looking for a company that was aggressive, innovative, and ready to break out—a company that was expecting a lot from me and willing to back my efforts.

3) I expected to be in a position where I could learn and where I would feel challenged.

4) I expected to be a part of a winning team in pursuit of excellence—a team of change makers.

5) I wanted the challenge of effectively leading, coaching, and developing my direct team to play an integral part in the company's success.

6) Happily, I joined the company, and now, almost a year later, I was ecstatic to share that not only did the company meet my expectations, but so did my colleagues.

I encouraged everyone to take a good look around at the incredible team that he or she was a part of, and then I thanked everyone for listening.

Relieved to be finished with my speech but still feeling very nervous, I fumbled to grab my pen from the podium and literally threw all of my notes up into the air. They fluttered to the floor as I awkwardly made my way back to my seat.

As I sat down, the vice president to my left stoically looked straight ahead and whispered—that was great!

I exhaled.

Our president and fearless leader took the podium next. He graciously thanked me for my speech and then asked everyone to be patient for a moment as he had to pick up some very important pieces of paper—my notes!—off the floor.

He continued by saying that my speech had summarized the reason for the meetings that week. I had stolen his thunder but that was okay. He said he was overwhelmed when he looked around the room during my speech and saw that others felt the same as I did.

In closing, he referred, again, to the idea of expectations. As a company, our expectations were in sync, and he was proud to be heading into the busy season with the best team ever.

I exhaled louder.

If you really want to be a successful employee, or hey, if you want to be successful as a company: you need to have detailed expectations from both the employees' and the employers' perspective. It's important to have not only common goals and plans but ideals as well.

The excitement of opportunity and challenge inspires us to push for greatness.

When I was first learning to golf, chipping the ball onto the green was a challenge for me. I was out of control and inconsistent. My alignment was off, too, and I swung every shot around and to the left. I just didn't know what I was doing. I took some lessons. The trick was to get the feel of tossing the ball: knowing the weight and speed required. It was explained that you chip the ball up into the air and then it drops and rolls. There is the basis of what is expected, and now you have to practice.

When you know what is expected, you know what you have to do! It's important!

I mention this because, a couple of weeks ago, a friend of mine told me about a conversation she had with one of her employees. She was sitting in her office when this young girl, fresh out of university, knocked on her door and then abruptly demanded to know why she hadn't been promoted yet.

My friend was totally taken aback. In her mind, the "new girl" in the office had neither impressed nor disappointed her. She was too new, and nobody really knew what she was even capable of, let alone whether she would be considered promotable.

Expectations!

It's important to know what is expected and then know how to deal with what is expected.

The importance of a code of ethics

A great way to instill the value of expectations and communicate them is through introducing a company code-of-ethics policy. This helps set the right tone as well as the right expectations from the get-go with every employee.

Because I feel so strongly about this, I'm actually including a sample for you to use. I have set it up the way that the code-of-ethics policy is set up in my company. It relates to the treatment of people first and foremost, which is always the best approach. Then it deals with the fusion of people and company vision. This is the fundamental basis of establishing a sense of corporate community.

The code-of-ethics playlist:

o Treat your colleagues, family, and friends with respect, dignity, fairness, and courtesy.

o Pride yourself in the diversity of your experience and know that you have a lot to offer.

o Commit to creating and supporting a world that is free of discrimination, harassment, and retaliation.

o Have balance in your life and help others to do the same.

o Invest in yourself, achieve ongoing enhancement of your skills, and continually upgrade your abilities.

o Be approachable, listen carefully, and look people directly in the eyes when speaking.

o Be involved, know what is expected from you, and let others know what is expected from them.

o Recognize and acknowledge achievement.

o Celebrate, relive, and communicate your successes on an ongoing basis.

The year when I took the lessons to improve my chipping, I chipped six balls ranging from ten to twenty-five yards, off the green, straight into the hole. It was amazing.

Herein lies the value of the lesson; we all need refreshers now and then, as I have never chipped as well as I did that year. We need to know what is expected to make the shot or succeed, and we need to practice what is expected so that we can clearly make things happen on the course and in our careers.

Risk vs. Reward

The 13th Hole - **Empower yourself and others**

Use your Machiavellian flair for the positive.

If that subtitle made your head snap back, don't worry. That's exactly what I did when I first heard the term "Machiavellian flair." It was when I received the results of a management-profile review from my new employer.

It was a mandatory employment requirement for all senior management and was intended to reveal whether you would be effective in the position that they had hired you to fill. I passed the audition, as they say, but I was intrigued by how they were using the term "Machiavellian." It means trying to achieve what one wants in a cunning and underhanded manner. Since that didn't sound good to me then (and it still doesn't), I had to figure out whether having a Machiavellian flair was in fact a good thing or not.

At the time, I was twenty-four, juggling long hours at work, being a young mother, attending night school to work toward completing my CMA (Certified Managerial Accountants) program, and trying to get ahead. I was working hard to get what I wanted, but I wouldn't say that I was cunning about it! I had just upgraded my career, going from a business manager of a small publishing company to controller for a large national manufacturer, but I was very careful not to be underhanded. In my resume and in my interview, I had undoubtedly spoken highly of my abilities, work ethic, and achievements, because I wanted the job!

When I was hired, I remember thinking, "Now all I have to do is do what I said I was capable of doing."

Some may say that I bluffed my way in to this new position, as I was young and green, but the way I see it, if you know you can do the job, where is the bluffing? Can being cunning be confused with being confident?

At that time in my life, I knew I was confident and competent, and that empowered me. I had stretched emotionally and intellectually as an individual, and I thrived on encouraging others to do the same. Stretching here meant warming up, moving farther each time in small, easy steps, and becoming more flexible overall in any or several aspects of life. I love the sense of stretching out and into new challenges. This new challenge was exactly what I had been training for after all.

Today, I recognize Machiavellian flair as a truly positive workplace mind-set. Forget the "cunning and underhanded" meaning; my best alternate definition would be "achieving a sense of empowerment." It's your knowing "what you bring to the table" and that you are the safe bet. It's about knowing that you are the one who will take charge and get results!

I always think that, although I love my life as it is, there is a whole world of experiences out there waiting. There are opportunities hidden at every turn, and you have to explore them all no matter how exhausting that may be. Every opportunity deserves a look!

Tips for empowerment

Have a voice. Have an opinion about things that are important to you.

Be heard. Speak up and make your thoughts known.

Have Influence. Use persuasion to help others understand your views.

Be involved. Step up and take part in what is happening around you.

Understand the vision. Recognize and buy into opportunities.

Encourage innovative thinking. Support fresh ideas and thought processes.

Demonstrate respect. Show support and recognition publicly, with a physical congratulatory handshake or an embrace.

Delegate responsibility. Share responsibility and relinquish trust to others. Release control of projects and spread decision-making authority around.

Be flexible. Encourage risk taking and be tolerant of failures.

Good employers set the stage for empowerment and watch for those that excel. Take, for example, having the confidence to delegate. You have to take a risk and trust that the person you are handing the reins to can handle things on your behalf and in your absence. This is setting the stage; there is opportunity and there is trust. Then it is up to the employee to accept this challenge and run with it.

Trust—especially competence-based trust—is a behavior, and any behavior can be learned.

Take time to observe your fellow employees in action. Observe the ones that you see as being empowered. You will probably find that there are many competent people in your workplace. They will be able to manage the tasks before them competently, even though they approach problems differently than you would. They simply get things done.

Trust based on motives rather than competence is created when you believe that others' intentions and values are closely aligned with yours. The more you trust their motives, the more assured you are that they will handle situations as you would. This being said, the employer intuitively feels more at ease with those whose motives are in line with his or hers.

Although competence-based trust is a straight-forward measure, motives are often intangible and tend to fluctuate. Therefore, trust relationships based on motives are rare in business and only tend to develop once competence-based trust has long been established.

The bottom line really is that most employers tend to rely on their management skills and their instincts. They trust their gut, since they know that it has brought them to where they are today. In addition, they trust those that come across as being empowered and up for the challenge.

As an employee, entrepreneur, or employer, empowerment is the excellence that opens the door to success.

Contained exhilaration is not nearly as exciting as its release...so accept challenge!

What excitement do you have to share with the world?

Risk vs. Reward

The 14th Hole - **Be proactive**

Are you up for this challenge?

If you take just one concept from this book, I hope it is this one. Being proactive is about the single most important thing you can do for yourself at work. Being proactive means meeting deadlines, actively eliminating whatever might get in your way so that you are unstoppable!

Whenever you are put in a position where you have to depend on others to get work done for a deadline for which you are responsible, you need to take on a proactive role in managing the overall progress so that you can ensure that things are done right and on time.

Again, this is like going to the driving range. You work on practicing and mastering proactively so that you don't waste strokes on the golf course.

Being proactive, however, has another important byproduct. By being proactive, you in effect challenge complacency. In today's tough marketplace, being proactive is not only crucial for survival, it ultimately paves the way for companies to reinvent themselves in order to stay competitive and to succeed.

The last quarter of 2009 marked the end of the worst recession seen for as many as sixty years. Fortune 500 companies have faltered and crashed, and literally hundreds of thousands of people have become displaced from what they once thought were stable and secure careers. The resulting financial uncertainty has taken us to our knees, as we have watched all that we have worked for in our lives devalue and, in some cases, disappear forever.

Nevertheless, tough economic times breed new and inventive beginnings. Businesses are reinventing themselves and aggressively rising from the ashes. They are focused, streamlined, and embrace technical innovation and efficiencies in order to forge ahead and meet today's business challenges.

As an employee, you need to be always reinventing yourself, finding new ways to improve your skills, bettering your position by finding ways to make yourself indispensable to the company—in other words, being proactive.

Crisis has always been and will continue to be the strong initiator of successful change programs in business. It is important to recognize, though, that change can also be effectively management driven.

If you want to be a good business leader, you need to proactively challenge the status quo and strive to stay ahead of your competition. You need to know what your customers want and effectively deliver those desires back to them. Employees, managers, CEOs—everyone in the company is involved in branding your company as superior within your industry.

Challenge complacency in the workplace.

To be more successful in business, it is vital to challenge the complacency that happens at all levels in a company. Businesses strive to become and remain viable while employees strive to become and remain invaluable. Here is a list of ways I have found helpful for me to take a stand against complacency and continue being proactive. As you read through this list, consider the impact of each item from both the employee's and employer's point of view.

Know your competition:

Gather, manage, and honestly represent information regarding your competition. Be prepared to accept how you stack up against them so you can define where change is required.

Value all sources of communication:

Dissatisfaction and problems as communicated by management and front-line people are needed to identify information regarding weaknesses and threats to the business. It doesn't matter whether you agree with what you are being told. What matters is that you are willing to realize that there is always value in what others perceive to be crucial and detrimental to the business. Sometimes you will be able to take what is communicated at face value and, sometimes, you will need to dig deeper to get to what change is required.

Market and promote change:

Create the opportunity for continual dialogue about where change is required in order to stay ahead of your competition and deal with problematic risk and exposure issues learned from the first two areas listed above.

Set high standards for yourself:

When you set high standards for yourself, you see yourself functioning at a high level. This generally creates dissatisfaction with the current situation and forces change, as long as you have a formidable career strategy and a well-laid-out and attainable implementation plan. This is where good benchmarking comes into play.

Remember that complacency blocks change. When you are too comfortable, you can't see what needs to be done. Being proactive blocks complacency and can give you an edge in the marketplace.

It is always important to understand your underlying motivation for being proactive and know how to communicate that motivation in such a way that you create a sense of importance and urgency.

Define the motivation that leads to being proactive.

So now we know why it's important to be proactive, and we know how to challenge complacency in the workplace, but how do you kick it all into high gear? You find your motivation, what it takes to get you ramped up and ready to recognize and avoid workplace hazards.

o   Desire to improve, whether in quality standards, product quality or offering, customer service, and/or sales performance.

o   Desire to feel more confident, directed, and comfortable that your business is headed in the right direction.

o   Desire to make changes that you feel or know are necessary as part of a high-level corporate vision.

o   Desire to create a sense of urgency to drive real change and get results.

Productivity and the effects of the recession

NOTE: Although the following section is primarily directed at employers, employees will benefit from reading it, as they will better understand what they should expect during a recession and, furthermore, how they can facilitate the process of working through the ripple effect of new challenges to be faced.

Even though this won't always be an issue for all readers of this book, as I write, "recession" is still rampant. There have been some dire fallout consequences to many companies, even those that had been thriving. During a recession, where layoffs and cost cutting run rampant, morale and productivity suffer. Uncertain times leave employees feeling helpless and fearful of losing their jobs.

So, here, the challenge is to be proactive and promote productivity in your business during any economic downturn. Here are some constructive ways to encourage and develop focused company efforts:

1) Have an open-book policy. Involve your employees and ensure that they understand the business, its finances, and how they can affect the bottom line. Show them fixed costs and profit numbers. Let them see that when the sales volumes drop to a certain point, losses quickly occur.

2) The managers among you can establish workable and attainable business benchmarks, which can be published and posted throughout the company. Clearly identify how the company is performing. You may think that you are giving up too much information, but in fact, you will minimize the effects of uncertainty within your key staff.

Usually, in times of recession or instability, the weak move on, but the fighters step up to the plate. If a downturn in business generates a better overall team within the company, there will be recognizable benefits moving forward.

3) Be direct and straightforward in all communications. Explain the rationale for changes and layoffs. Be serious, to the point, and clear.

4) Communicate well and be succinct. Say only what needs to be said to make your point.

5) Make changes and show improvement quickly. Use the "make me believe" principle to keep focus and attention on your overall strategy.

6) Reconnect with your customers and let them know that they come first. There should be no selling, just communication. Show appreciation for their business and your joint successes. Too many companies lose track of who their customers really are. When they do, customer service becomes lip service. Not all the fancy "partnering" jargon in the world can repair the damage done.

7) Be visible by keeping your doors open and walking around the office. You have nothing to hide when circumstances are out of your control.

8) Show employees that they are valued and that their work is important for the company's continuance and eventual recovery. Provide incentives that will kick into play when the company's performance improves.

9) Celebrate and communicate all successes. New business, new clients, improved sales, and cost reduction are necessary and important.

Wasted strokes, like missed deadlines, are preventable and costly.

You can tap greater potential, thrive through challenges, and take a front-row seat to success by being proactive. Once you have documented, analyzed, and encapsulated pertinent information about your business and have generated a revitalized corporate vision, you need to create urgency and put your plan in motion.

For employees, increased momentum toward a revitalized vision will instill a renewed sense of purpose and a higher morale level among moti-vated employees. Confidence in the business and its leadership, coupled with the infusion of new ideas and streamlining of processes, will produce a more efficient focus.

For managers and employers, incorporating an effective and dynamic ongoing communication that includes moderate detail of successes, no matter how small, will inspire morale, allow you to retain valuable employees, and ultimately boost productivity during a downturn in sales.

The same process effectively incorporated as a normal course of business will set you up to become an industry leader. Being proactive is crucial to attaining growth. It helps you excel at showing continued value to your customers and will keep you aware of upcoming opportuni-ties and challenges to be faced in the future. Businesses that thrive and grow are continually reinventing themselves. They use technology, improved efficiencies, and relevant market data to their advantage in order to stay current and vital.

If you can't see and calculate sustained change and improvement...it didn't happen!

Risk vs. Reward

The 15ᵗʰ Hole - Learn from the change-ready company

Which came first: the change-ready company or the change-ready employee?

It's one thing to think proactively and even act proactively, but it's another thing entirely to put that thought process into play and invoke change on a large scale. Companies that effectively do this on a consistent basis are recognized as being "change-ready." These dynamic companies are high functioning, responsive, and almost fluid in their approach. Working at such a company offers great opportunities for those who thrive on change.

Change-ready companies offer variety and challenge, and they encourage entrepreneurial spirit. As the overall objective of being change ready is to see documented change, those employees and departments responsible for that change are both accountable and noticed. If you perform well, reward and recognition will follow. It can mean instant gratification for your efforts.

Without forward motion—you will lose control.

Change-ready companies are those that are able to recognize, respond, and adapt effectively. They recognize shifts in key markets. They respond by making decisions, and then they adapt their focus in order to capitalize on opportunities. They strive to be more effective and react faster than their competitors to take advantage of potential new market opportunities.

If your company needs a boost and you really want to generate change, you need to communicate the necessity or perhaps urgency for that change. You have to set the stage and create an environment that is conducive to change.

Knowing that the change-ready company evolved through the efforts of change-ready leaders and teams, you can no doubt see how much there is to learn by immersing yourself in such a dynamic and challenging process.

Being an active participant in the fluid mode of a change-ready operation can put you face-to-face with authentic, modern-day mentors. They are the mentors that are worthy and awe-inspiring.

Change occurs in waves as markets, technology, and customer wants change. You can't just coast along. You need to communicate change. The following is a sample plan:

How to communicate change:

When planning, announcing, implementing, and communicating a change initiative, it is important to note that there is no perfect formula. For most of us, change is uncomfortable. You can throw a plan of attack out there detailing who should do what and when and make some progress, but long-term habits are not easy to change.

The best place to start is to define what change is required and why. Be specific and direct.

Know what results you want, both from the change initiative and from the communication program or tactic.

Knowing and understanding how people react up-front can add to your chances for success and curb the potential for damage control after the fact.

Share information with your team as soon as possible. There's a real dilemma in public companies where investor communications are the number one priority. Whenever employees hear about a reorganization or merger through an outside source, they feel disconnected and unimportant. This exposes the company to unnecessary turmoil, as employees lose their sense of job security and loyalty.

You can't communicate too much significant, substantial information. Effective change requires longevity. A change effort starts with an announcement but then needs a substantial allotment of time and effort, ultimately to build and create a complete change cycle.

Use a variety of communication routes that continually reinforce change. Repetition is of key importance here.

Not much in the world ends up being the same as it started out, unless of course it had a very short life cycle.

I can't help but refer back to the idea of strategizing in golf, knowing how to work the ball using the arsenal of fourteen weapons you carry in your golf bag. Most recreational golfers have their favorite clubs, the ones they are most confident with, the ones that they can hit well. Perhaps out of the fourteen clubs, they only feel reasonably proficient using six clubs: the driver, the 5 wood, three of the irons, and putter.

That means that they do not feel proficient using the other eight clubs—that's more than half!

I once read an article that stated that you should never have a favorite club. The point was that, if you practiced hitting all of your clubs at the driving range, then you should be able to hit them all well, so there would be no favorites!

This is the biggest lesson to be learned from the change-ready company and its processes. There is a definite need to be proficient and use all of the weapons in your arsenal—in this case, all of the business knowledge and expertise, current market indicators and trends, technological advancements, and recognizing ever-changing customer needs and preferences.

In today's global market, successful businesses are aggressive, innovative, and open to change. Employees who succeed in the workplace adopt that same attitude for themselves. Ensuring that you are change-ready in today's economy is simply par for the course.

Shoot for the biggest and boldest impact possible. If you need a full corporate makeover—do it. Moderation is just not going to cut it.

Risk vs. Reward

The 16ᵗʰ Hole - **Cultivate team spirit**

We = power

My dad once said, "If you have a problem, share it with someone who you think can help you. If nothing else, your problem will be cut in half."

There is a lot of truth to this. This is the essence of and strength behind working as a team.

Building the right team and cultivating team spirit is one of the most powerful business strategies anyone working in any kind of company atmosphere has available; yet, it is one that is often overlooked.

Working successfully as a team is hard work. It takes a strong team leader to maintain a respectful and open work environment. Individuals with different personalities, skill sets, and agendas need to feel that they are part of the team and learn to work together to achieve a common goal.

The right team needs to include people who are willing to work and be a part of the team. It also has key people who have the ability to create a sense of positive culture. They aren't necessarily the leaders, but they are the coaches. Their knowledge base is vast and includes the following:

o   Relevant expertise for the project, directive, or opportunity

o   A full range of perspective and discipline to get results

o   Sufficient credibility so as to be taken seriously

o   Strong leadership and interpersonal skills

o   Ability to forgo personal interests that could potentially interfere with corporate goals

Finally, a good team leader will recognize the team's efforts, as well as the individuals'. In this way, he or she can build a high-performance team that is confident and challenged. A good team member will be ready to actively jump in with both feet and follow the direction as set out by the team leader. Although the team leader sets the tone and acts as a guide, the team in its entirety is the power.

Steps to building the power team

Whenever a team is needed, a well-thought-out plan is also needed to motivate the team into working together and cultivating a sense of team spirit and enthusiasm. Here are the basics:

o Start a new team by organizing an off-site meeting. A break from the everyday work environment usually sets people at ease, and they are then more open to change and meeting new team participants. Keep the meeting loose and creative and watch how the group interacts. Set aside time to brainstorm and strategize, but your focus should be to allow the team members to get to know one another.

o Group leaders should acknowledge individual achievement during group meetings, as well as compliment the team as a whole for working well together. By providing positive recognition and feedback, with relevant examples, the group leader can build a sense of respect and unity within the team.

o When acknowledging strengths within the team, also make an effort to highlight new ways in which those strengths can be used that could further benefit the performance of the team.

o Ask the right questions and listen to the answers. People excel when they are doing what they enjoy and what they do well. Know your team.

o If someone is not making the cut, revisit why he or she was initially selected to be part of the team. Your work environment may have stifled the very characteristics you admire. You may need to refresh your overall approach.

o Know that every action has an equal and opposite reaction. That being said, if an employee has a specific weakness, what is his or her opposing strength? Find it and bring it to light. Encourage and cultivate this newfound strength.

o Cross train everyone. Cross training instills a sense of teamwork, but it also allows employees to explore other roles within the company. They may be better suited in a different position based on their skill sets. This will lead to improved overall job satisfaction.

o Recognize and highlight interim successes with a team lunch or food brought into a meeting. Such mini-celebrations are great morale boosters.

o Use benchmarking or progress techniques to monitor the productivity of the team. If there is a lull or dip in performance, consider an activity to recharge and refocus the team. Sometimes a simple, inexpensive break can energize and boost a team's productivity.

o Celebrate the completion of a project in some manner. Recognition is paramount.

I've got that club in my bag!

I was playing golf on a team with one of my buddies in Florida. On a par four, I smoked the ball from the tee, but when it hit the ground, it rolled right and went into a sand bunker. We were playing best ball and playing skins (a hole-by-hole wager where the lowest score wins; when there is a tie, the win carries over to the next hole, until there is finally a lowest score). We decided to play from my ball, as it was closest to the green. The next shot, however, involved hitting out of the bunker and over a cluster of palm trees in order to reach the green.

I boldly shouted out, "Hey, no problem. I've got that club in my bag." My friend laughed and said, "Great, we need it, bring it on!" We both warmed up for the shot and chanted, "Yah, yah, we can do this!"

At that point, through my peripheral vision, I saw a couple, well within earshot, walking along a fitness trail toward the green. They had heard my "club in my bag" boasting and the two of us joking around and getting totally psyched for the shot. I turned beet red and thought, "Boy, I had better have that shot in my bag."

I took my 7 iron, angled it for more loft, and swung deep into the bunker to pop the ball up and over the palms and land on the green that I couldn't even see.

I took a deep breath and took the shot. The ball cleared the palms in the right direction and we ran out to watch it drop and roll within three feet of the pin. The couple walking by watched the ball land too.

Whew! We birdied the hole (a birdie is a score of one under par—in this case, scoring 3 on a par four) and I was redeemed.

Ultimately, all of the silliness and boasting that day was about us having fun. The fact of the matter was that I did have that club in my bag, meaning that I was confident that I could make the shot and did. We high fived and laughed our heads off. We came out to play and were having some success!

Encourage and celebrate the team.
It's where your power comes from.

Risk vs. Reward

The 17th Hole - **Take the initiative to lead**

A good leader is both forceful and believable.

On the 16th hole, "Cultivate team spirit," we discussed the team as a whole within the workplace and how to build the effectiveness of that team. A tried-and-true program revolves around positive reinforcement, powerful team-building rituals, and constructive, focused direction. This chapter, in effect, follows the same train of thought but goes further, focusing on how to take the initiative to lead to a broader scale—from the assertive, progressive employee, to the team leader or manager, or even as an employer or leader of leaders.

No matter what your position within the workplace, you can actively take the initiative to lead. You can focus on achieving an upwardly mobile transition within your organization by understanding and embracing those traits common to successful leaders. The primary role of a leader is to lead, and in order to lead, you need to stand out, command attention, and demand respect. Leaders usually have a definite vision they are committed to and passionate about. They know how to plan and build the right team to set process in motion, and they have the ability and desire to see projects through to the end no matter what hazards may come into play. Successful leaders, in effect, achieve force by demanding credibility, commanding attention, and being able to use their interpersonal influence to transform workplace staff, colleagues, and even customers into their devoted entourage.

Demanding credibility is relatively straightforward and easy to attain if you are perceived as being knowledgeable about the subject, issue, or directive of interest. Commanding attention is also relatively straightforward if your intended audience perceives that you are similar to them, which directly helps them relate, feel comfortable, and want to listen to what you have to say. Ultimately, though, the essence of creating leadership force comes from the energy that you put forth, as well as the enthusiasm and vitality it displays.

A good golfer's métier is his or her golfing skill. A great golfer's métier is his or her golfing skill, coupled with the mastery of good sportsmanship, rendering him or her an ambassador for the sport.

When you think of a leader that has created force in golf, I am certain that Arnold Palmer immediately comes to mind. He has become a living icon that exemplifies not only the physical abilities, endurance, and dedication required to excel in the sport of golf, but also integrity and professionalism through his lifetime of excellent sportsmanship.

The stronger the team, the stronger the leader

Leaders don't stand alone, however. They have an established and vast knowledge base backed by competent people resources. The relationship between the effective leader and his support team is definitely symbiotic; they build on one another's strengths and build together.

Skill in interpersonal communication tops the list for successful leadership.

A good leader knows the value of sincere and regular affirmation. To good leaders, the process of building up others is of key importance. If you're an employer or a manager, take, for example, the performance review. It is important to highlight strengths and articulate how to improve constructively. Challenging people to be better a bit at a time is part of the overall positive business culture that needs to be created and cultivated on an ongoing basis. If, on the other hand, you are an employee trying to climb the ladder, you can learn a lot from successful leaders. They can motivate and inspire, and they can challenge you. Respected leaders make excellent mentors.

Reflections of the successful leader.

When we think of those that we deem to be good leaders, a multitude of varied traits come to mind. Generally speaking, effective and respected leaders are vibrant and strong. They are usually active and most often confident, hardworking, and credible. They also have excellent communication skills and are able to talk the talk in a manner appropriate for an ever-changing audience.

They are positive when they speak and deliver messages that are crisp, direct, and easy to understand.

Respected, effective leaders are able to motivate, challenge, and retain good employees—the team. They attract highly talented people and create a sense of group competence within the organization.

Some leaders are viewed as being courageous. They bend the rules, push the edge of the envelope, and choose to be open to new or abstract ideas. These leaders can never settle for standing still. They are always looking for a better way. For them, taking the easy route is not easy. Taking the easy route for some is not even an option.

It's sometimes easy to believe in a course of action at the time, only to find a week later that it's not a good course of action after all. With honest, straightforward communication, this sort of miscalculation will be addressed. Company expectations in conjunction with the overall vision will be revisited, and then a new strategic direction will evolve. Authentic leadership is evident when the level of commitment, influence, and follow-through has shown documented results.

This is how entrepreneurial companies and large corporations can stay connected with the ongoing pursuit of the companies' core vision. They develop a structured, comprehensive, and dynamic corporate strategy, and then hire a forceful and believable leader to orchestrate its success.

As much as good leaders need the entourage of effective and strong team players, they also need to know how to deal with potential opposition and encourage participation. Give everyone repeated opportunity to voice concerns, ask questions, and offer ideas. Address all concerns and follow up with answers and updates. The more people are involved in the change process, the fewer you'll have walking out the door or, worse, staying and sabotaging your efforts.

Effective leaders try to build rapport with different key personalities within the organization. It's important to have everyone on the same page, so to speak, but this is often difficult due to the fact that you usually deal with a large volume of people, each with his or her individual agendas and motivations that may not always coincide with that of the organization. The best you can do is work toward building a common base of shared knowledge, tolerance, and respect.

The following list details potentially disruptive personality types and how best to deal with them.

The Boisterous Power Seeker:

These people try to steal control and power from others that they perceive as threatening to their stature within the company. They are always positioning themselves, so they appear as the most valuable and most knowledgeable. They interrupt, intimidate, and antagonize.

What to do: Calm with praise.

In most cases, boisterous power seekers are really seeking recognition. Deep down they know that they are bright and talented, but they need to be complimented and stroked on a regular basis and made to feel more secure.

By acknowledging these types' expertise in a specific area and seeking their opinion, you re-inforce their sense of real worth and value. This calms them completely as all they really wanted was some attention.

The Retentive Information Hugger:

Also insecure about power, information huggers don't want to share information that will help you do your job, even though it may ultimately affect the company. They will give you pieces of infor-mation but are quite comfortable withholding the most important bits.

Huggers want to maintain control of important information, as they perceive themselves to be powerful and more important. They feel no re-sponsibility for any bad decisions made because of information they have withheld.

What to do: Make them get to the point.

The best approach to talking with information huggers is to make them disclose what they know by asking a series of clarifying questions. Keep asking questions until you feel certain that you have retrieved everything that they know on the matter.

The Enthusiastic Attention Grabber:

Enthusiastic attention grabbers are so enthusiastic about their work and the current project that they blurt out answers and ideas without thinking them through. Sometimes their sheer enthusiasm can influence others toward buying into their ideas, rather than taking the time to come up with a decisive and well-thought-through solution or program, which could result in disaster.

What to do: Slow the process and focus on details.

Have an itinerary, stay on point, document input that is constructive and ultimately going to assist in everyone reaching the common goal of getting the job done, and minimize the effects of internal saboteurs.

The self-generated leader

Leaders are self-made—home grown; it's a learned skill and it's a choice made!

———

We all take on the role of leader at different times in our lives outside of the workplace, with our families, in sports, in school, in day-to-day life. Now you just have to practice what you already know in the workplace.

When you channel your desire and willpower toward continuing to learn through education, training, experience, travel, and self-study, you catapult yourself into the forefront. When you take the initiative to lead, you become the self-generated leader.

Although this book specifically deals with targeting success within the workplace, the workplace itself is quite a different place as you move from one industry to the next. That being said, the most valuable leadership skills are also quite different as you move from one industry to the next, although the basics remain the same.

Where a real estate agent will excel by being knowledgeable within his or her market, he or she will take the initiative to lead if that agent is excellent in communicating, providing feedback, and following up with his or her respective buyers and sellers.

Where builders may excel at providing quality built homes at a good price, they will take the initiative to lead if they are continually on or ahead of schedule and known for getting things done right the first time around. Their reputation will grow through word of mouth.

It's all about being committed to and passionate about your vision of excellence within your industry. It's taking the initiative to lead the way, striving to be the best at what you do.

When you are destined for greatness, it shows in everything you do. It becomes you. Greatness becomes you.

Risk vs. Reward

The 18th Hole - Succeed in the workplace

Living the dream—your dream!

Back in '73, I was in an enriched math program in middle school. My teacher was one of my older brother's friends, and he was hot! I would even go so far as saying that, back then, he was undoubtedly the hottest man in the world next to Kurt Russell.

Back then, I was shy and, of course, totally mesmerized by him. He would chat with me now and then and inquire about my brother, and I would stutter back my awkward, nervous reply.

One afternoon, though, he stopped me in the hall and asked me a rather unusual question. He asked, "Am I challenging you?" I didn't know what to say. He continued, "I just wondered if I am challenging you. I know that you are smart."

The hottest man in the world had just told me that he thought I was smart!

From that point on, I felt that I was smart! A huge thank you is definitely in order.

There are building blocks that come from all directions. We use them to form a foundation and then build our own personal road to success—our own pursuit of what success means to us. Along the way, small successes grow and spill over to other parts of our lives.

It's like pulling out your driver one day and hitting the ball twenty or thirty yards farther off the tee than you usually do. What do you know? First, that you *can* do it and, second, that you have made a breakthrough. Your hard work and dedication have paid off, and now you will move forward at a new, higher level of expertise. Your expectations of yourself and your abilities have been elevated.

Hmmm. You have seen firsthand that you have the "driving" force to succeed. Sorry, guys…

So, what does being successful mean to you, and what traits do you possess that will enable you to rise to the top? The following are the main success traits covered in this book.

Success starts with the right attitude.

The right attitude screams out, "I am amazing!" It says that you are a winner, a contender, a star. Your attitude is your choice. You can self-assess, recognize your strengths, and build on them, and you can recognize your weaknesses and revamp them. Remember that self-perception is an extremely powerful resource. Self-assess, shift your attitude, and change in order to reveal a new and improved version of yourself. Choose your attitude wisely and succeed.

Successful people develop winning habits.

Success isn't achieved by doing something once. You need desire and motivation to push yourself into high gear. You need the drive to forge ahead, and you need to develop winning habits that can guide you through challenges. Winning habits help us focus and realign. They are the consistent and persistent reflections of your person, demeanor, and credibility. Even in times of urgency or crisis, winning habits can help you through, as you inherently know what to do and how to do it.

Successful people thrive on learning.

Being ready and willing to learn is one of the most incredible and powerful things you can do for yourself. Think of it as investing in yourself. The more you learn, the more you are *able* to learn. It's the whole concept of opening up your mind, being aware, and understanding.

Successful people share their potential.

Everyone has a skill or talent particular to him or her. Some choose to share their excellence, while others may choose to hold on tightly to their uniqueness and withhold it from the world, while still others may not even recognize that they really have something worth sharing.

Either way, whether you know it or not, you have potential.

You can be aware of your potential and even be passionate about it, but if you aren't willing to force it into play, your potential can flat line or remain dormant. It's your choice.

When you do know that you are particularly good at something, though, and then communicate and exude confidence, you appear charismatic. You are charming, attractive, and magnetic. It's not what you say or how you say it, but rather the way your person interacts with others. It's the whole package. It's about being open to giving or sharing yourself with the world. This is success.

Successful people are motivated and they break down barriers.

Motivation always intrigues me. We know that materialism really packs a punch in motivating people, but you can't dispute the value of the raw motivation that develops when people decide to have children. Your focus becomes redirected toward putting others first. You want to be able to provide an environment of security and safety. You want your kids to have everything—opportunities and choices. With this new outward focus, anything that may have been holding you back is now unimportant. At this point, it's not all about you anymore. No, now it's go time!

Successful people deal with stuff.

You can't dispute the value of making decisions—it's the whole "three off the tee" concept in a nutshell. Whether the decision is good or bad, things still get accomplished and you end up moving forward. The more decisions you make, the better. This really means that you are taking control of your life and your destiny. When you make a good decision, you win. When you make a bad decision, you learn from it, regroup, try

---

again, and *then* you win. It's living your life; it's no excuses; and it's no regrets. It's successfully taking charge of your life!

Successful people are confident.

It's all in your head. You just need to remember this simple fact. Remember and relive all of your successes no matter how small or trivial they may seem. Success is success. There are no limitations, and there are no borders. Reliving your successes builds your confidence, and this spills over to all that you do in your life.

Successful people accept challenge.

Keep your eye on the ball! If you can't see it, you can't hit it. This is true of challenge. If you don't put yourself out there, take some risk, and accept challenge, you will never be ready to grab hold of challenge and turn it into opportunity. Have you heard the saying, God hates a coward?

Successful people have a strong character.

When I think of someone as having a strong character, the following traits come to mind: drive, energy, determination, self-discipline, willpower, and nerve. He or she has a strong moral fiber and an impetus for doing the right thing. It's often said that, while many are capable of doing things right, someone who is truly successful will aspire to do the right thing.

Successful people understand positive influence.

Positive influences are by nature very similar to successes and life lessons. You relive them and make them a part of who you are. You play fair, you expect to work hard and to improve, and you focus on communicating well and developing solid relationships and understanding.

Successful people have a game plan.

Self-direction and self-determination are going to get results. By being flexible, proactive, and versatile, no matter how many challenges or forks in the road you encounter, you will eventually find your way. The undeterred always make their way.

Successful people are team builders.

The trick to team building is to practice as a team. Have a commonality of direction and focus and become results oriented. The successful team leader, having excellent communication skills, can guide and coach the team toward a common goal while, all the time, encouraging the team effort. If you don't encourage people to work and practice as a team, they are not a team but rather just a group of people.

Successful people have passion.

Sometimes finding your passion in life is a challenge. It can be illusive and ever changing and, even if you do figure it out, it may always be just out of reach. Many people will weed out the pursuit of their passions early in life, as there may be too much risk involved or perhaps not enough opportunity to make a comfortable living.

Pursuing your passion in life, however, is the trail that leads to finding yourself. It's your place of surrender and comfort—where you can shut out the rest of the world, if only for a short time, and live in the moment. If you have taken the career path that undoubtedly pays the bills, don't lose track of your passions. Carry them with you for when the time is right!

Successful people have presence.

People that have presence are very intriguing. They draw our attention and respect. There is an essence of being mysterious and yet at ease while having the ability to lead, charm, persuade, inspire, and influence others.

They are set apart from others, and we are compelled to acknowledge them. What exactly is their draw? It can be mystique, exuberance, personal appeal, magnetism, extreme charm, or even positive energy.

Although presence can be defined in many different ways, ranging from projecting unusual calmness, exuding confidence, or attaining the right level of assertiveness, the bottom line is that those with presence command attention. Now, if you could ever bottle and market "presence," that would be an instant success.

Successful people play the part of being successful consistently in all that they do.

People make judgments based on your profession and what they expect a person in that profession to be like—from family life to material possessions to behavior.

For example, one might expect that a good financial investor would have an expensive and impressive house, thus exemplifying their success. On the other hand, a business owner may be expected to contribute to the local community, while a lawyer or doctor may be expected to behave in a respected and trustworthy manner. It's not enough to play the role of success just at your workplace. It has to be *you* that is successful, and it must show consistently at home, work, or play.

Successful people make time.

Whenever you try new things, you learn. The knowledge is not contained. It spills over to other aspects of your life without your even realizing it.

Take golf, for example. Aside from the regular skills, such as developing an effective, reliable swing and basic course management, you are exposed to the impact of nature. You interpret wind direction and speed, dew and moisture on the greens, and even how temperature affects your body. If you are cold and tensed up, you're going to throw the motion of your body off.

I like to be busy all the time, and I have no problem making time to try new things. When I paint or take photographs, I pay attention to reflection and movement. When writing music, I strive to stimulate emotion and inflection. All of this awareness and these thoughts spill over and make me more effective in other parts of my life.

For me, making time is an easy choice. I say bring it on—the busier the better!

I'll sleep when I'm dead— until then, it's game on!

There is a painting hanging on the wall in one of the bedrooms in our house. We bought it for my dad when he retired. An old man with scruffy gray hair and stubble on his face is leaning back in an old fishing boat not far from shore. Across from him sits a young boy that we assume must be a grandson. They are fishing. The sun is brilliant and bouncing off the ripples in the water. As the young boy eagerly stares at the point where his fishing line disappears in the water, the old man looks on and smiles gently.

The painting is simply called "Success."

Success is the self-fulfillment of dreams.

Play to Win

The 19th Hole
Educated Optimism

The 19th hole is the fun after the game. It's grabbing a beer, having some laughs, reliving the good shots and, no doubt, being razzed about the bad ones. It's time to look at your scorecard, see how you played, and get a game plan for what you will do differently the next time out.

Think about the "work hard—play hard" principle. For the recreational golfer, golf is the "play hard" part. You work hard at the workplace and may even work hard at the golf course, but as a recreational golfer, you aren't planning to become a pro—you came out to have fun!

I enjoy the competition and sportsmanship of golf. I work my ass off to get better, get some exercise, and enjoy the day. I may not score well, but I *love* the game.

In the past, close friends and colleagues have labeled me a workaholic and encouraged me to get away from the office. Taking time to learn to golf seemed like an awesome way for me to do just that. I have had a lot of fun on and around the course, and I am actually quite proficient at chilling out with a beer on the 19th hole. Ahhh…

Game over! Game on!

One of the most important concepts to incorporate and practice in your day-to-day life is that of realizing the necessity to challenge yourself continually in one or many sectors of your life. There are times to work hard, times to play hard, and times to do whatever it takes to make it all work for you. Think about how diversified and chaotic our lives become over time. We play several different roles at work and at home, enjoy successes, deal with failures, regroup, and get things done. We chase the ideal of attaining success and balance in our lives.

When you push yourself to learn, you are really taking time to invest in yourself. There is a sense of enlightenment and confidence. You grow more and more knowledgeable about what is important to you, and this affects your view of the world—you see the glass as half-full, rather than half-empty. I refer to this as educated optimism. You like what you see, which is a direct result of your own efforts. You feel positive because of your knowledge. Whether developed through education or experiences, or both, you have developed a sense of educated optimism. It is an ongoing process and an important ingredient in building a successful life.

The funny thing is, if you ask most people if they are genuinely happy with all of the results in their life, the truthful answer is often no. Why? Usually, because they feel they don't have the time to pursue their dreams and interests. They can't seem to find the time to do what they want. They may long for new experiences and challenges, and want to attempt and try new things. They may even yearn to resurrect an old dream, but for some reason, they never make the time and, therefore, feel they are missing life.

Well, take it from the workaholic. Each one of us can probably find at least one hour of time each day that we are wasting. My suggestion is to make the effort to dedicate a chunk of time every single day to reflect on where you are in your life and where you see yourself in the near future while focusing on self-development.

If you are unhappy with something in your life, you have the ability to change it, take control, change your behavior, and improve.

Think of it this way: You can Sudoku yourself to death, or watch hours of TV, or you can open your mind to learning new things.

For me, learning is a passion. I am always reading. I *love* thick hardcover books about business, psychology, travel, and art, and I spend hours sleuthing information on the Internet. I'm an information junky. I want to experience and try everything. I want to sail the world, drink in culture and philosophy, learn different languages, and continue to grow as a person.

Somewhere along the line, my passion for learning turned into a life habit. It's what I do. It's not difficult and, as hectic as my life gets; I always make time to learn.

This kind of self-study works and it turns you into an educated optimist. You are mentally stimulated; you know a little about a lot of different things that you are interested in, and you have a lot to talk about. You have effectively rendered yourself interesting.

This form of personal development helps you grab hold of what works well in your life and enables you to see where things could be better.

If you are looking for a good place to get started, look at what you like or love to do. Think about what you used to like to do but can no longer find the time. Then make the decision to make the time. Make time for you! Again, invest in yourself!

Everything that you do in life spills over; when things are working in your work life, it spills over to your home life and vice versa. When you look forward with educated optimism, it shows in all that you do. Perhaps educated optimism is the ultimate positive attitude that drives success in our lives.

Avid golfers creatively practice their sport! They check their grip as they grab the handle of a broom, and they test how well they calculate distance as they walk their dog! You might say that avid golfers always keep their game in play—even when off the course.

Glossary of Golf Terms

A

"A" position – The "A" position is that position which allows the best approach for your next shot.

Address – Address refers to the golfer's position when preparing to make a stroke (hit the ball).

Address the ball – Addressing the ball means that you are in position and prepared to hit the ball. At this point, your main concern is whether you are properly aimed at your intended target and whether you are ready to take your shot.

Alignment – Alignment refers to the direction that the body and club are in when in the address position—for example, when you line up your body drawing a swing direction parallel to the target with your clubface square to the target.

Approach shot – The approach shot is a shot where your intended target is the green.

At the turn – At the turn traditionally refers to having completed the first nine holes of golf and getting ready for the back nine or last set of nine holes to be played.

B

Back nine – The last nine holes (ten to eighteen) of an eighteen-hole golf course.

Ball position – Ball position is the position of the ball relative to a player's stance and the target at address. The ball is considered to be "forward" in the players' stance if the ball is nearer the front foot or "back" in the player's stance if the ball is closer to the rear foot as relative to the target.

Best ball – Best ball is a match where an individual plays against the better ball of two, or the best ball of three.

Birdie – A birdie is a score of one under (less than) par for a hole.

Bunker – A bunker is a hollow or valley of some kind, usually filled with sand. A bunker is also known as a trap or sand trap.

C

Chip – A chip is a shot played from around the green usually played with a pitching wedge or a sand wedge.

Course management – Course management or game management is the use of strategy to emphasize strengths and compensate for weaknesses in order for the player to make his or her way around the golf course as efficiently and effectively as possible.

D

Driver – The driver is also known as the 1 wood. It is the most powerful club in the set and used to achieve maximum distance from the tee.

Driving range – A driving range is an area, separate from the golf course, designated for hitting practice balls.

E

Errant shot – An errant shot is a shot that leaves you in long grass, under a tree, in loose tangled brush, or in the water.

F

Fairway – The fairway is the closely mown, proper route, between the tee and the green.

Fairway woods – Fairway woods 2, 3, 4, 5, and sometimes higher-numbered woods designed for use when the ball is in play after the tee shot.

These clubs are often referred to as fairway met-als today, as they are more commonly made of metal rather than wood.

Fringe – The fringe is the collar of slightly longer grass around the closely mown putting surface of the green.

Front nine – The front nine or front denotes the first nine holes (one to nine) of an eighteen-hole golf course.

G

Green – The green is the most closely mown and smooth area of the course, which is specifically prepared for putting. The green is also referred to as the putting green, putting surface, and the dance floor. When you are on the green, you're dancing!

Golf course – A golf course consists of a series of holes, usually two sets of nine, where each hole consists of a teeing ground, fairway, rough, and other hazards, and a green with a flag or pin, and cup, all designed for the game of golf.

Grip – A grip is the handle of a golf club, usu-ally covered with rubber or leather. Alternately, a player's grip refers to the method of holding a golf club properly.

H

Handicap – A handicap is the average difference between a series of a player's scores and a set standard.

Hazard – A hazard is any bunker (a hollow or valley of some kind, usually filled with sand) or water hazard (ocean, lake, pond, river, ditch, etc., usually marked with either white or red stakes or lines), even a sloped bank, that can hinder you from making par.

Hole – The hole, 4-1/4" in diameter into which the golf ball is played.

Hole-in-one – A hole-in-one is a score of one on a hole. The perfect shot!

I

In play – In play officially refers to when the ball is hit from the tee and comes to rest anywhere on the course, not out of bounds. Informally a ball that is in play is playable.

Iron – An iron is a club with a head made of steel or iron with a relatively narrow sole (footprint), with varying lots, and numbered one through nine including a variety of wedges. That being said, the most common array of irons carried in a set of golf clubs is the 3 iron through pitching wedge. Many golfers add a sand wedge to the mix and/ or a 1 or 2 iron, a gap wedge, or a lob wedge.

L

Leader board – A leader board is a scoreboard showing the top performers in a golf tournament or competition.

Lie – The lie is the position in which the golf ball comes to rest.

Loft – The loft is the angle of the clubhead relative to the shaft of the club from the frontal plane. Loft produces more of less height and makes the ball rise.

Lost ball – A golf ball is considered to be lost if after a five-minute search, it cannot be found. The player is penalized one stroke.

M

Match play – A match play is a game of golf where you compete on a hole-by-hole basis.

Mishit – A mishit is any stroke that is not shot solidly.

Mulligan – A mulligan or mullie is a do-over. A player takes a second attempt or replay of a shot when he doesn't like the result of the first.

Muscle memory – Muscle memory is a phrase referring to the nervous system's ability to memorize, or automatically reproduce, a well-practiced motion.

N

Nineteenth hole – The nineteenth hole or 19th hole is the bar or lounge after the round of golf.

O

Out of bounds – Out of bounds or OB, is an area that is not part of the course and on which play is not permitted. White stakes usually mark the out of bounds area.

P

Par – Par is the standard number of strokes in which a scratch golfer, a golfer with a zero handicap, is expected to complete a hole.

Par for the course – Par for the course is the standard number of strokes in which a scratch golfer, a golfer with a zero handicap, is expected to complete eighteen holes.

Penalty stroke – A penalty stroke is a stroke added to the player's score, for a variety of reasons such as a lost ball or an unplayable lie, in accordance with the rules of golf.

Pitch – A pitch or pitch shot is a relatively short, lofted shot designed to land softly and without a lot of roll.

Pitching wedge – A pitching wedge, P, PW, or W is a lofted short iron.

Practice green – See green.

Practice range – See driving range.

Pre-shot routine – A pre-shot or pre-swing routine is a procedure or consistent sequence used as preparation prior to hitting a golf shot. There are three basic considerations to keep in mind: Am I properly set up; am I properly aligned; and is my ball in the correct position? You need to take a minute to visualize the shot from behind the ball and perhaps even choose an intermediate spot in front of the ball, in line with your primary target, to use as an alignment aid.

Putt – A putt is a shot generally hit with a putter that is intended to make a ball roll on or from just off the putting green.

Putter – A putter is a club with a fairly straight face and very little loft used for putting.

Putting green – See green.

R

Range – See driving range.

Recovery shot – A recovery shot is a shot that will set up the succeeding shot—a shot that has a good lie so that you are in position to make your next shot. A recovery shot is played to extricate oneself from trouble after an errant shot.

Recreational golfer – A recreational golfer is an amateur player who plays for recreation or fun and, therefore, uses a more relaxed interpretation of the rules of golf.

Regulation – Regulation or being on the green in regulation, means playing your ball onto the green in the prescribed number of strokes as determined by par or simply par for the hole, less two strokes for putting.

Round – A round or round of golf is actually eighteen holes, broken up into two sets of nine.

Rough – The rough is the area of less kempt grass and vegetation bordering the fairway. Playing from the rough generally entails more difficulty in attempting to make clean contact with the ball.

Rule #27 – Ball lost or out of bounds, states that if you lose a ball hit from the tee, you can hit from the tee again or drop a ball two club-lengths back from where your ball exited the fairway. Either way, your score is one stroke from the tee, plus one penalty stroke for the lost ball. In other words, you are now hitting three—one stroke for the lost shot, plus the other two from the tee, thus the term "three off the tee."

S

Sand Trap – See bunker.

Sand wedge – A sand wedge, sandwedge, or sand iron is a lofted club with a flange specifically designed for use in the sand.

Sandbagger – Sandbagger is a euphemism for a liar or cheater. This refers to a golfer who lies about their ability in order to gain advantage over opponents in a match or wager game.

Score – A score is the number of strokes taken on a hole or course.

Scorecard – A scorecard or card is a preprinted card usually provided by the golf course, used to record and tally scores during and after a round of golf.

Scratch – Scratch is a zero handicap.

Scratch player – A scratch player is one who is expected to play the course in par.

Set of clubs – A set of clubs includes a maximum of fourteen—usually four woods, nine irons, and one putter.

Set-up – see address.

Short game – The short game in golf refers to approach shots to the green and putting. Some people think of the short game as anything inside of one hundred yards and yet others think of it as shot on or in the immediate vicinity of the green.

Shot – A shot or stroke in golf refers to both the act of swinging a club with the intention of striking the ball and then the past tense of striking the ball.

Shot planner – See pre-shot routine.

Skins – Skins is a hole-by-hole competition or wager where the lowest score wins. When there is a tie, the win carries over to the next hole, until there is finally a lowest score.

Slice – A slice or banana ball is a faulty shot that curves left to right in the air (right-handed player).

Slope – The slope of a golf course is a rating of the relative playing difficulty of a course for players who are not scratch golfers.

Stance – Stance is the player's position when the feet are set, in alignment, ready to play the ball.

Straight up – Playing a game of golf straight up refers to playing a competition or wager where no handicap is used to adjust the players' scores.

Stroke – See shot.

Stroke play – Stroke play is a game of golf where you compete against others based on your total score for eighteen holes.

Swing – A golf swing is the player's physical motion used to make a stroke.

Swing thought – A swing thought is a short catch phrase intended to help the player keep his or her mind in the game and focused on making the shot.

T

Target – A target is that location where you intend a shot ball to lie or finish.

Tee – The tee is the flat, sometimes raised, area from which first shots at each hole are played, as well as a small device used to set the ball up above the ground in preparation for taking a shot.

Tee Shot – A tee shot is simply the first shot on a hole where the ball was shot off a tee.

Three off the tee – If a ball hit from the tee is lost, out of bounds, or unplayable, the player is penalized one stroke and then tees off again, hitting a third shot.

Trap – See bunker.

Trust your Swing – When you trust your swing you are confident in your ability to make solid and clean contact with the ball.

V

Visualize the Shot – When you visualize the shot you are able to use mental imagery to see the shot required.

W

Water hazard – A water hazard is any sea, lake, or pond, whether it contains water or not, usually marked with either yellow or red stakes or lines.

Wedge – A wedge is a sub-set of irons, shorter in length, with significant loft and generally used in short game play. Various wedges include the pitching wedge, sand wedge, lob wedge, third wedge, and utility wedge.

Wood – See driver and fairway woods.

Work the ball – To work the ball means to deliberately shape or curve a shot to your advantage.

Note to the Reader

Watch for the next book in the *3 Off the Tee* series of motivational self-improvement books.

Make it Happen will send you on a current, timely, and thought provoking journey of self-discovery.

Break down the big picture, figure out what works for you, and develop the right mind-set and social finesse to achieve personal success.

You can, *Make it Happen!*

About the Author

Lorii Myers is an empowered employee turned entrepreneur. Her over three decades of business experience include a wide variety of career challenges: business manager, controller, senior manager, and business owner.

She believes that you should aspire to learn from those who inspire you and therefore she was careful to choose her early employment opportunities well. She worked for entrepreneurial companies, owned or managed by formidable entrepreneurs. When asked what she learned? Myers is quick with the answer – "The **right attitude** is everything!"

Myers left the security of employment to fulfill her own sense of entrepreneurial flair in her early thirties. Because of her personal quest to explore every opportunity, she brings a wealth of knowledge and experience to this book. Her challenge to you is to "come out to play, take on the world, and make success yours!"

Your Targeting Success quest begins now!

**Please feel free to contact
the author and share your success stories:
Lorii@3-Off-the-Tee.com**